MW01122543

From Pilot Knob to Main Street

*A Collection of Recipes and Stories
from Yesterday, Today & Tomorrow*

by

Ethel S. Tucker

*For Lisa
Happy Cooking
"Enjoy"

Love
Ethel
May 2005*

authorHOUSE™

1663 LIBERTY DRIVE, SUITE 200
BLOOMINGTON, INDIANA 47403
(800) 839-8640
WWW.AUTHORHOUSE.COM

First published by AuthorHouse 04/20/05

ISBN: 1-4208-2960-2 (sc)
ISBN: 1-4208-2959-9 (dj)

Printed in the United States of America
Bloomington, Indiana

This book is printed on acid-free paper.

I DEDICATE THIS BOOK
TO THE MEMORY OF MY HUSBAND
THOMAS NUNN TUCKER
AND HIS SISTER
DOROTHY TUCKER FRAZER

Acknowledgements

Alan and Doris Stout
Keith and Julie Stout
Imogene S. James
Allison Mick-Evans
Tony Nichols
Joseph Brazell
Rachel Byford
Dulcie Hardin
Brian R. Hunt
Susan Yarbrough

Introduction

It was in the year 2000 that I began seriously writing this book. My husband, Thomas Tucker, encouraged me, as he enjoyed the food that I served him. Then he died August 24, 2001, so the book was put on hold.

My nephews, Keith and Alan Stout, and families, Bill and Bohn Frazer and their families, as well as friends, have done the testing and tasting of the menus and recipes for me. Sometimes they were more complimentary than others!

During my long lifespan, I have had the opportunity to see a lot of the United States, Mexico, Canada, and to take a trip to the Orient. Being exposed to the different cultures, beauty and the food, I can truthfully say western Kentucky is the most ideal place to live. And I'm thankful that I live in Crittenden County, and "On Main Street" in Marion.

I have lived a full life, and I am very thankful. The Lord is so good to me to let me live and have the good health - physically, spiritually, and mentally - that I have! As this book comes off the press, I will have just turned 87 years of age. It is my hope that both young and old will benefit from and enjoy the recipes, menus, bits of wisdom, history and stories. I love my home, but most of all, I love my Lord Jesus Christ, my family, and especially you! Read "From Pilot Knob to Main Street" and enjoy - that's my prayer!

Table of Contents

Chapter One - History

The following pages cover some incidents in my life that serve as history for family and friends. Compiling this book is not meant to be boastful but to thank the Lord and praise Him for the long and full life I've had and to thank my many friends.

The Beginning

It was on Thanksgiving Day, November 29, 1917, that I arrived into this big world on Pilot Knob in the central part of Crittenden County, Kentucky about three miles north of Marion. My parents, Burt and Lizzie Stout, and a sister welcomed me, nurtured me and spoiled me. The big snow of 1917 and 1918 began falling on that same day, and it snowed every day for two months, blowing and drifting up to eighteen feet I have been told!

I was an experimental baby of that time. Mother's milk did not agree with me. Aunt Mollie, the midwife who came to live with us (as was the custom), would talk by phone to Dr. Frazer who had delivered me. The snow was so deep that he could not make a house call to Pilot Knob in his horse and buggy. He told Aunt Mollie to try giving me diluted tomato juice, and as I began to grow and thrive he called me his "experimental baby."

First Christmas of Remembrance

Mother and Papa were so pleased, so the story goes, that the crops had been better and they felt Santa Claus could splurge! On Christmas morning there was a big beautiful doll with dark brown hair in my rocking chair. I think I had just turned four and was still small in my desires. Tears streamed down my face and Papa said, "Honey what is the matter?" I said, "I didn't want a big doll I wanted a little one." Both parents were disappointed, for they thought they had what would make for a big happy Christmas. Papa called his

1

friend in town who ran the grocery store where he traded, and it was open. So Papa hitched the buggy up with his favorite horse and came to town on Christmas Day and bought a little twenty-five cent doll for me. And I was happy! I did play with the big doll as I got older, and it made the move to town later on. This could be a lesson for the parents and Santa Claus.

Box Supper at Brown School

While living on Pilot Knob, the children of the neighborhood attended the one room Brown School. It was about two miles on a dirt road and across the field from our house. Fund raisers at rural schools in the 1920s were Pie Suppers and Box Suppers. I was a bit artistic even in my younger years, wanting to make something pretty out of our limited resources. My mother, Lizzie, let me make a crepe paper flower and a bow for the box I was taking to the big Box Supper at Brown School. The boxes were auctioned off to the boys and men to the highest bidders. Low and behold, because of the beauty of my box, it brought the highest price. As I remember, it brought $1.30. I was seven years old, and the red headed man and I ate the contents of my box with careful supervision from my parents. It consisted of fried chicken, deviled eggs, pickles and homemade cookies.

Fourth Sunday in May

Mother was famous for her fried chicken. She fried it in a black iron skillet, and I do it the same way in the same skillet!

The fourth Sunday in May was always the all day church service with dinner served under the shade trees at Crooked Creek Baptist Church, the oldest church in the county. Papa would hitch the mules to the wagon and take us all to church. We would get dressed up in our best Sunday clothes and shiny black patent leather slippers. When we would get home, we would take off our shiny slippers and rub them with cold biscuits and put them in the tissue paper-lined boxes until next Sunday. Each year the three Lizzies - Lizzie Stout, Lizzie Enoch and Lizzie Fritts - would carry their dinner out of church and spread it out on two benches turned facing each other. The following is what I remember eating there: Baked ham, fried chicken, corn light bread, homemade yeast bread, corn pudding, pickles, apple pie and angel food cake.

Papa Buys a Car and Learns to Drive

In the spring of 1926, Papa bought a new Model T Ford car with icing glass curtains to put up when the rain or cold weather came. He bought it from Tucker and Foster, which was in the same location of the present Gilbert Funeral Chapel and the former Tucker Funeral Home. He hired a neighbor, Mr. Charlie Conger, to teach him to drive. The first of July he took the family on a big trip for the times, to visit mother's brother and family in Tennessee Ridge, Tennessee, then on to Nashville to show us children where he proposed to mother. I remember that the highway was gravel most all of the way, which we thought was great, since our road was dirt. Papa became ill on that trip, and he had to hire men to drive us home. Few people had learned to drive. One man drove us to Hopkinsville, Kentucky and he knew someone there who could drive us on to Princeton and Marion. In Marion, my cousin Bill Stout drove us on home to Pilot Knob. Papa died just a few days later.

1926

1926 is a year that I remember so well - some bitter, some sweet. The year marked my father's death, our move to town and my entering a new school. I well remember on October 26, 1926 that mother took us children to the dedication of the 'magnificent' Fohs Hall. She told us that it was making history! Little did I know as an eight-year-old child that I would play in a piano recital on that big stage a few years later, nor did I think that in 1935 I would walk across that big stage to receive my diploma from Marion High School.

3

Our Big Move to Town

Papa's sudden death changed plans in a hurry. My young mother, forty-five years of age, had children from first grade to Rosa Lee, a freshman in high school. Mother was concerned about getting Rosa Lee to Marion to high school and Howard and me to Brown School. Papa and a neighbor, Mr. Bee Cloyd, took turns taking the Pilot Knob kids to and from school in the wagon when the weather was bad.

After much praying, planning and talking to advisors, mother decided to rent out the farm and move to town. This we did about the time school started. During all the frustration of the last week on Pilot Knob, Howard, the little timid-six-year old, fell out of a peach tree and broke his arm. In addition to starting a new school in a classroom full of strangers, he also had the pain of a big, heavy plaster cast on his arm. I was in the third or fourth grade in the same old grade school building near the Marion Post Office. Rosa Lee went to high school in the Hayward building and Fohs Hall.

We all walked to and from school as well as home for lunch. If the weather was bad, we took our lunch. There were no school buses or any school lunch programs.

Ethel Stout, age 12, and Howard Stout, age 10,
after the family's move to Marion.

Life in Town

When we moved to town, Mr. & Mrs. Henry Stone took us under their wings. They had visited us on the farm and bought strawberries, and occasionally just came to visit. They had one of the first cars in Marion. The Stones owned a dry good and variety store. The store was located on the Court Square. They hired mother to work in their store.

Ethel Stout and Lizzie Stout in front of Stones
Dry Goods Store in Marion, 1938.

When I reached the age of twelve, Mr. Stone hired me to work on Saturdays for fifty cents a day. Store hours on Saturday were from 8:00 a.m. to 10:00 p.m.

This was a learning experience for me. After finishing high school, I worked full time during the summer. Then I went to college for a year in McKenzie, Tennessee. After that year, I had a full time job working for Mr. & Mrs. Stone. His health began to wane and he was not able to assume management of the store. He gave me half interest in the store. I became the buyer/manager and my mother and I were the main salespeople. I was always so pleased to show and sell fabrics. Back then most everyone either made their own clothes or had them made by one of the several dressmakers in town. I still enjoy sewing and handwork.

Ethel, Howard and Rosa Lee Stout

Rosa Lee Stout's nursing photo

Children Do Grow Up

Rosa Lee, the oldest of us three children, became a nurse. She took her training at Deaconess Hospital in Evansville, Indiana. When Rosa Lee finished high school, she wanted to be a nurse. But mother felt it too hard a profession and encouraged her to go to teachers college and become a teacher. That was the "in" profession at the time. After teaching two years and being so unhappy, mother realized she had made a mistake. So Rosa Lee, who was a very dedicated nurse, got to fulfill her life dream. After working at Deaconess Hospital for a few years, she and another nurse decided to go to California, where they thought the grass was greener. She married Ralph Pedersen, who worked in the Redwoods. They reared three children, Burton, Norman and Suzy. Rosa Lee lived the rest of her life in California and is buried in Ft. Bragg, having died in 1967 at the age of 54 of cancer.

Howard Stout during World War II

World War II came along and Howard was drafted. He served in the European Theater and was wounded severely. He had married Imogene Crider before the war had begun. They married October 9, 1939. After his return from the war, he and Imogene lived a while with Lizzie, and that's when Imogene started making the angel food cakes that she is still famous for today. Their two sons, Keith and Alan, still have her angel food cake at the top of their list of desired desserts.

Thomas Nunn Tucker, 1938, our first date at Smithland Cemetery

Ethel Stout Tucker, 1938, our first date at Smithland Cemetery. Thomas carried this picture with him overseas during World War II while serving on the USS Sanctuary, a hospital ship.

Our Marriage

Thomas Nunn Tucker graduated from Marion High School, also in 1935. We had dated some after high school. On the first date, he took me to Smithland Cemetery. He was brought up in the funeral business so this was not unusual. We looked at monuments of some of his relatives. We took pictures of each other in front of the Haynes-Given Mausoleum. He carried that picture of me all the time he was in the Navy.

When he first proposed, we were going to wait to marry until the war was over. Then it became a typical war wedding. The time kept being moved closer and closer for him to leave, and he wanted to marry before he had to ship out to sea. So we married March 27, 1943. He had a ten-day leave. We had the wedding at the home of his sister and brother-in-law, Dorothy and Robert Frazer. We went on the train to Asheville, North Carolina for our wedding trip.

In spite of the rushed wedding, there were many nice parties in town for us. I still have many of the wedding gifts. They were mostly crystal, China and silver which were in vogue at the time.

A few months after our wedding, Mr. Stone and I sold the store inventory, and I joined Thomas. He was still stationed at Great Lakes Naval Station.

Our First Thanksgiving

We were very fortunate. When I arrived at Great Lakes, we went to Waukegan, Illinois and were able to rent a very small efficiency apartment. Many Navy couples and families lived there.

I soon got a job as a clerk in a department store. I worked in the stationery department, and monogramming was very popular. I learned to use the monogram press for both stationery and leather goods. Jack Benny was from Waukegan, and I had the opportunity to monogram a pipe case for a friend of his when he came for a show at the naval station.

On our first Thanksgiving, we could not come home because we had used our gas ration stamps and could not get enough gas to come home. So we invited a Navy couple to eat Thanksgiving Dinner with us. I cooked all morning, and while we were eating dinner, the kitchen wall caught on fire. Dinner was interrupted while the firefighters put out the fire. The fire kind of saved the day for me! I had baked a chicken, made a pie and cooked dressing in the oven and it got overheated. Carving facilities were limited, so I sliced the chicken before dinner. It looked like there was not much meat on the platter, so I put the bones on the bottom and the slices of chicken on top. The platter looked pretty good, even though I could not find any parsley for decoration and instead used canned fruit. After we were all served, I sat the platter on the stove. Pretty soon Thomas asked me to pass the chicken again. That's when I discovered the fire. He always would say, "there is plenty more in the kitchen." When I turned to get the platter of mostly bones is when I discovered the wall on fire.

The landlord was pretty upset. She said that too much cooking had gone on and that I should not do that much cooking anymore.

Thomas Nunn Tucker,
1944, at Crane Naval
Ammunitions Depot

Ethel in Crane,
Indiana, 1944

Navy Days

Thomas was soon transferred to Crane Naval Ammunitions Depot in Crane, Indiana. He was stationed there about a year working in the hospital laboratory. I got a job in the records office. He was sent out to sea, and I continued to live and work at Crane until the end of the war. My mother came and lived with me part of the time, as well as a cousin, Gertrude S. Brown, who worked in the office with me. Thomas sailed on a new hospital ship, The US Sanctuary. They brought the wounded survivors from the atomic bomb in Nagasaki, Japan to a distribution center in Korea.

Thomas was discharged in November 1945, and we returned to Marion.

We lived with his parents the first year and then moved into an apartment that his father owned, rent-free for about a year.

Our first home – 251 West Bellville Street, Marion

Our First Home

About two years after we returned to Marion after World War II, we bought our first home. It was the home that Thomas' grandparents had owned and were living in when Thomas' mother was born at 251 West Bellville Street. Tommy and Mary Tabor now own it. We sold it to them when we moved to Main Street.

It was when we lived there that I began cooking big family dinners. This is also when I began thinking of the importance of presentation of the food and how to make the most attractive dishes.

*New Year's Day 1960 – Mary E. Stout , her niece Christine
Ware and Thomas Tucker at Bellville Street house*

*Party at Bellville Street house – John Barabe , Georgia Cochran,
Anita Guggenheim, Bob Crooks and Nancy Westberry*

Thomas' sister, Dorothy Frazer, also liked to cook. Before her health began to take its toll, we had many parties together and usually had them at our house. We always loved to have company. When our friends would have out-of-town guests, we found that was always a good excuse for us to have a party. Sometimes we would have as many as twenty for a sit-down dinner and more if it was an open house or a cocktail party. Domestic help was plentiful and not too costly. Food was also less costly at that time.

Cissy Gregg was the food editor for the Louisville Courier-Journal and had many usable recipes. I have several of her recipes that I've been using for more than fifty years and still have at least one of her cookbooks in our library of cookbooks. Thomas would sometimes read cookbooks as if they were fiction.

Community Affairs

All my life I have had a desire to help others, and one might say I was community minded and interested in bettering the community. I remember that very soon after World War II, the American Legion and its auxiliary were very active locally as well as all over America. When I was president of the auxiliary nearly sixty years ago, child welfare and community service were the two areas most needed locally, and there are still needs today.

The first home that the Legion had was upstairs over The Peoples Bank. It had a large meeting room, kitchen and restrooms. For several years it held many community affairs meetings there and many dinners were served by the auxiliary. Then they bought the home on the hill known as the Dr. Nall home. It is now owned and occupied by Mr. and Mrs. Bill Greenwell. For fund raisers, we served dinners and then we had several style shows along with lunch, and they were always a sellout.

Woman's Club of Marion's Derby Party fundraiser

Another civic group that I've enjoyed being a part of for a long time is the Woman's Club of Marion. Its home was also built in 1926 and still serves as a cultural and social center.

When Fohs Hall was no longer needed for a school, a community group bought it for $1 and Fohs Hall, Inc. was formed in 1980-1981. I was at the first meeting and have been on its board since then, having served as treasurer for ten years during the time of restoration.

Fohs Hall, Marion's cultural center

Fohs Hall Board of Directors – May 29, 2001. Kneeling, Daryl Tabor, Alan Stout, Doug Sullenger; standing from left, Malcolm Hunt, Mary Conrad, Barry Gilbert, Judy Winn, Jim Carter, Ethel and Thomas Tucker, Linda Schumann and Nicky Porter.

Annual meeting, Community Arts Foundation in 1997 when Ethel retired as resident director. Presentation made by then CAF-president Rebecca Johnson.

In 1988, Fohs Hall Community Arts Foundation was formed, and I was the first Resident Director. The nearly ten years as director was a thrilling time for me. Having new experiences and opportunities in all forms of the arts broadened my scope of life and I hope for the whole community. The biggest effort accomplished during that time was publishing the Crittenden County History book (two volumes). Thomas helped with it, as he was known as the county historian. The last county history book published was about one hundred years ago. The Arts Foundation is a non-profit organization, and the sale of these books helped with operational expenses and bringing entertainment to the community.

Business Days
1951-1982

After the death of Thomas' parents and his partner, Thomas purchased the survivors' interest in both the funeral and furniture business. This is when I became active in the business. I served an apprenticeship and took the state examination and became a funeral director. Then in the 1950s the trend for home decorating services was on the rise, so I took a design decorating course and graduated from New York School of Interior Design. We made a small section of the furniture store for the decoration shop. A seamstress, Gwendolyn Matthews, was hired to help make curtains, draperies, etc., and with the help from the men who worked for us, I taught myself to reupholster furniture. With this, the first decorator shop, Tucker Interiors, began to grow!

In 1970, we sold the furniture and appliance business to Johnson's. We made a major restoration to the building and made a modern funeral chapel on the first floor and Tucker Interiors moved to the second floor.

Eulanda

Living at Eulanda

About the time of retirement in 1981, Thomas had two new opportunities to help keep him busy.

Eulanda, the property he owned near Dam 50, needed some repair work, and he decided to put an addition on it. At about the same time, he inherited a part of our present home on Main Street. He bought the other heir's part, and it had to have major restoration.

For about two years while the work was being done on the Main Street house, we lived at Eulanda and rented the Bellville Street house.

Eulanda had a lot of room, and we enjoyed having company there. Our friends from town enjoyed coming to the country. Many times we would have 19th century settings, using kerosene lamps. We had a turnip green and hog jowl supper with corn dodgers. The town people really liked the menu as well as the patchwork cloths on the tables.

Family dinner at Eulanda. Robert Frazer, Linda Frazer, Sherry Frazer and Thomas Tucker

Dinner party at Eulanda when Ethel's nephew Burton Pederson and his wife Dawn visited Thanksgiving 1982. Dawn, Earl James, Imogene Stout James and Burton

Dorothy Franklin and I were co-hostesses for a church women's circle meeting. She came early to help and stayed all night. The next morning she told me that it sure helped her to spend the night in the country!

As the deer population grew and we seemed to have more night meetings and social functions in town, we decided it was time to move to town. We sold Eulanda and moved to our present home on Main Street.

Living on Main Street

Thomas and I enjoyed living on Main Street, and even though it's a lot of house for me, I continue to enjoy it since his death.

We were away for one Thanksgiving and all the other Thanksgivings and Christmases we had a dinner on the day or close to it for family and friends. Some of the menus and recipes we usually served are in this book.

Reception for Bill Winstead – Mike Croghan, Becky Croghan,
Imogene Winstead, Bill Winstead, Edna Gowans and David Gowans

While I was the director of the Arts Foundation, we opened our home to the board and guest artist Bill Winstead, who plays with the Cincinnati Symphony, for a reception following a Sunday afternoon performance at Fohs Hall. The menu for it was similar to one in the menu section of this book.

*Tom's 85th birthday - Earl James, Thomas
Tucker, Perry Chipps and Bill Frazer*

Twenty-four family and friends gathered for Tom's 85th birthday.

Tom's 85th birthday – Betty Sullenger, Earl James,
Thomas, Helen Springs, Perry Chips and Ada White

Guests at Tom's 85th birthday – Helen Moore, Robert L.
White, Earl James, Thomas, Perry Chipps and Ada White

On Thomas' 85th birthday, May 29, 2000, I had a buffet dinner party for twenty-eight friends and family. The menu for that dinner is also in the book. Of course he said I should not go to so much trouble, but he was pleased that I did. He loved every minute of it, and I'm so glad I was able to do it.

21

I love to bake and share! My happiest times are when I'm doing something for somebody, and I've learned that it does not have to be a big thing.

Thomas always loved to set the table, especially after retirement when he was home most of the time. Since his death, I find it hard to get the table set the few times that I've had dinner guests.

Our first Christmas season on Main Street, Thomas wanted us to have a widow's dinner during the time the decorations were up. He picked them up in two trips and after dinner, of course, he took them home. We had buried most of their husbands through the years. The women are all deceased now except May Flanery. Of course they all said that coming to our dinner party was the highlight of their holiday.

Katie and Logan Stout on Katie Stout's 8th birthday

Entertaining Children

We enjoyed having the children of nephews, neighbors and friends visit us.

On Katie Stout's eighth birthday, we had Katie and her brother Logan for an afternoon party. We gave her a toy ice cream maker. She and Logan studied the directions and made ice cream to eat with her birthday cake. They are the children of Alan and Doris Stout.

Katie Stout, freshman sorority picture, Murray State University, 2004

*Table set for Katie Stout and her family and friends
on commencement night, May 2003*

Logan Stout, Kirk Stone and Tyler Watson, Prom dinner, April 2003

Erica Guess, Logan Stout and Katie Stout,
children of Alan and Doris Stout

24

A few short years later, we had a dinner for Katie and some of her friends on Prom night. Logan and two of his friends, Kirk Stone and Tyler Watson, served the dinner for me. On commencement night, her family and out-of-town friends who came for her graduation had dinner with me. Now she is in her second year of college at Murray State, and Logan is a sophomore in Crittenden County High School. Their older daughter, Erica, is working in San Francisco, California.

Max Alexander

Max Alexander arrived at the home of Susan and Mick Alexander, at the north of our house, about the same time we moved to Main Street. We watched Max grow up and he just recently completed time in Afghanistan. Presently he is in the Army National Guard in active duty in Military Intelligence Special Operations. When he was very small, at Christmas he would always come lightly knocking on our door and hand us a package. Thomas would ask him what it was, and Max would say, "My mother wrapped it, you will have to open it to find out!" He has kept up the tradition. I served him brownies one time when he was visiting us. He told me that my brownies were almost as good as his mother's. He and Thomas had just eaten about four a piece. Thomas always kidded me when I made brownies.

Meredith Evans and Abby Whitney attending United Methodist Women's Christmas Coffee, 2001

Christmas Coffee, 2002 - Shelby Dunham

Women's Christmas Coffee, 2001 - Saundra Marie Winn, Savannah Peek and Amanda Wicker

Ryan, Matthew and Shelby Dunham, Christmas Coffee 2001

Christmas Coffee, Methodist Church Women, 2002
– Julie Stout, Ethel Tucker and Doris Stout

Christmas Coffee 2002 – Ethel Tucker, Jerry
Beavers, Dorothy Hughes and Dulcie Hardin

*Christmas Coffee 2001 - Louise Hamilton,
Imogene Stout James and Patsy Love*

Christmas Coffee 2001 - Micki Crider and Rebecca Johnson

It is such a delight to have some of the children of the ladies who come to the Christmas party that I host for the ladies of the Marion United Methodist Church each December. Some of them eat in the living room with the ladies and some prefer to eat at the kitchen table. They are always perfect little ladies and gentlemen!

Birthday party for Emily Owen, 2003

Emily Owen's birthday cake

At the Marion United Methodist Church, we have a program called "Adopt-a-Child." I adopted my good friend Emily Owen. On her ninth birthday, I had a party for the children of the church and some adult friends. They were served punch in silver punch cups and ate hot dogs, chips, baked beans and birthday cake at the dining room table covered with a linen cloth.

Jessie McDowell

Thomas and I had been living on Main Street about five years when Jesse McDowell, the daughter of Kim and Danny McDowell, arrived in the house on the south side. We watched her grow up so fast. Last year she turned sixteen and is now driving the family car. She is active in 4-H activities and enters items in the county fair and the Kentucky State Fair as well, winning many blue ribbons. She wanted to learn to knead yeast bread. We had several training sessions in our kitchen. She took some to the state fair that she made and won a blue ribbon for it. When she was about twelve, she brought us some "gooey butter cookies" with a recipe card attached to the plate. I'm sharing that recipe in the cookie section. Thomas thought they were 'Oh so good!'

Bill and Sherry Frazer's grandchildren – Tucker Frazer, 7; Maddye Mink 3; and Regan Frazer, 3

For some of the adults in the family I offer a birthday dinner with a menu of their choosing. Early in 2004, I offered the same to Tucker Frazer. He chose Lasagna and apple pie. Tucker and Regan are the children of Sharie and Bart Frazer. Bart is an attorney in Marion.

Maddye is the daughter of Sarah Ann and Jim Mink. They live in Frankfort and frequently visit Bill and Sherry Frazer. The three children are my great-great nieces and nephew by marriage.

Marion United Methodist Church

Marion United Methodist Church sanctuary

Religious Connections

I was reared in the Baptist faith. As a child, I attended Sunday school and church at Crooked Creek Baptist Church. When we moved to Marion, mother joined the First Baptist Church and I joined in my teenage years. That church, especially the pastor, did not sanction me marrying a Methodist, so I was excommunicated. In spite of this action, the pastor, Bro. Lilly, and all of that church family remained friendly to Thomas and me. When I married Thomas on March 27, 1943, I joined the Marion United Methodist Church and have been a member since. The Lord has led me to serve in several capacities of the church as well as to assist in the women's work. At that time, the title was the Women's Society of Christian Service. I served as local president as well as the president of the Henderson district.

Salad Luncheon, Madisonville District United Methodist Women – Mary Lou Chipps, Dorothy Renfro, Louise Hamilton, Lucy Leonard, Betty Sullenger and Ethel Tucker

In the early years, the women served many dinners and banquets for organizations and school functions. Until the Marion Country Club was built, the church social hall was the largest facility in town for such functions. Before the educational building was built in 1956, we used the old social hall under the sanctuary. That was when we cooked on the old coal range!

Now I'm one of the oldest members, having been a member over sixty years. I continue to enjoy fellowship with the church family and receive spiritual uplifting each time I attend a service (and I don't miss many!)

So you see, living over four score and seven years isn't all bad. The Lord has been so good to me and is still; that's why I want to share with you. I want you all to know the Lord as I do, and ask you to let Him come into your heart if you have not already done so.

I have faith and I believe that He will take care of me. I'm ready and willing to do what he wants me to do.

As the life expectancy continues to extend up the ladder, it means we will be living longer. It is important that we take good care of our bodies. We must eat well and stay as active as possible. I continue to ride my stationary bicycle every day!

It is with love that I bring you this message. "The mountains and hills may crumble, but my love for you will never end; I will keep forever my promise of peace." So says the Lord who loves you. Isaiah 54:10

Chapter Two - Helpful Hints

Food will brown faster and cook more evenly if it is not just out of the refrigerator; let it set out no more than 20 minutes.

Par-cooking means to cook food partially. You can par-cook by boiling, blanching, steaming or microwaving. I use the microwave to cut time in baking potatoes. Cook the potatoes in the microwave about 4 minutes for two potatoes and then transfer them to stove oven to finish baking.

I use a pinch of sugar and a pinch of salt in most everything. As an example, before sautéeing meats, sprinkle a tiny amount of sugar on the surface of the meat. The sugar will react with the juices and then caramelize, causing a deeper browning as well as enhance the flavor. Likewise, a pinch of salt in any dessert enhances the taste. Try salt in your next custard type pie filling and a few grains of pepper in any fruit pie.

For best results in breading foods, be sure that the food or meat to be breaded is very dry. Use eggs at room temperature and beat them lightly. If time permits, bread the food and refrigerate for about an hour, then let it set at room temperature for 20 minutes before cooking. I save my homemade bread heels and crusts to make crumbs. They brown better and usually taste better.

A sharp knife is safer than a dull one. Dull knives are more likely to slip off foods, resulting in cut fingers.

When preparing a lunch for work or school, freeze your drink carton or can and pack it in the bag with your wrapped sandwich. It will act as an ice pack to keep the food cold but should thaw by lunch time.

The ingredients for baking cakes and cookies should always be at room temperature. For pastry it is just the opposite, the ingredients should all be cold.

Muffins will come out of the muffin pan more easily if you place the hot pan on a cool, damp towel.

I think the secret to light biscuits is to handle the dough as gently as possible. Overworking the dough will make for tougher biscuits.

If you will sprinkle a thin layer of corn starch on the top of a cake before you ice it, the icing won't run down the sides.

When mixing batter, spray the beaters with vegetable spray before using them and the batter won't climb up the beaters.

If you are really having a big barbecue, for example 50 folks coming for a big get-together, this may help you. Start with 18 pounds of ground beef for hamburgers and 6 dozen buns, then 20 pounds of hot dogs and 100 buns. For the side dishes, it will take 2 gallons of baked beans, 1 ½ gallons of potato salad and 10 pounds of coleslaw.

Be sure the liquid going into your pie crust is ice cold. Ice cold sour cream instead of ice water will make a flakier crust.

People who love pies can save about 150 calories per serving by eating single crust pies and cobblers instead of two crust pies.

If you want to try something different, enhance cake flour by adding 2 tablespoons of corn starch to each cup of flour, sifting them together. This will produce a light, moist cake.

Spraying a small amount of Pam on your knife before cutting a cream pie with meringue will stop the filling and meringue from sticking to the knife.

To make easy chocolate curls, all you have to do is run your vegetable peeler on a chocolate candy bar.

To make pies with graham cracker crusts easy to remove from pan, dip the pan in warm water 5-10 seconds, then the pie will come out more easily.

Sprinkle sugar on the plate before you put a cake on it. This keeps the cake from sticking, and makes the bottom crunchy.

Baking apples, tomatoes or green peppers in well-greased muffin tins will help them hold their shape.

The kernels of popcorn that fail to pop can be put in the freezer overnight then they will pop when frozen.

Remove the smell of onions from your hands and cutting board with very salty water or some white vinegar.

When baking cakes, cut wax paper the size of the pan, spray pan with Pam and place wax paper in cake pan. Then spray paper with Pam a sprinkle with flour. Then add cake batter. After baking and as soon as you invert cake onto wire rack, remove wax paper. Crumbs come off with the paper, and it makes cake more smooth.

Chapter Three - Menus

When I plan to have a dinner, small or large, I start with the entrée and then think of what will be most compatible to taste and appearance. I think looks go a long way, not only on the dinner plates, but on myself (but that's another story). I try to have only one item on the menu with cream sauce.

I feel that so much fast food on the market may have taken some of the glamour out of the art of cooking and entertaining.

It is good to offer one new recipe on the menu. Do not be afraid to experiment, but at the same time, I would urge you not to try more than one new item, or undertake too much. You don't want to wear yourself down before dinner! When the main course is heavy and filling, I like to serve a light dessert such as fruit or sherbet.

I like to experiment with herbs and seasonings. I especially like sweet basil and rosemary. Thanks to Barbara Wheeler, I am growing these herbs in flower pots as well as parsley and cilantro! If a recipe calls for one teaspoon of a fresh herb, you should only use half as much of the dried herb. My motto: use sparingly and taste to see if more is needed. I also share some tips about garlic, which is so popular now and is so healthy.

Most every recipe listed in this menu section is printed in "From Pilot Knob to Main Street."

Baked Steak Dinner
Baked Steak
Sliced Baked Potatoes
Tossed Green Salad
Fruit Pie (Blueberry or Apple)

This entrée can be started earlier in the day, then baked for one hour before dinner, and the potatoes can bake at the same time.

41

Holiday Beef Tenderloin
Beef Tenderloin
Green Beans and Carrot Bundles with Squash
Mushroom Pie
Green Salad (assorted greens) with Poppyseed Dressing
Cherries Jubilee

When we had some out-of-town guests, I used this menu, for there is very little last-minute cooking. The beans can be done ahead, salad greens prepared early and the cherry sauce made ahead and add " jubilee" at serving time.

I find when I'm using commercial ice cream, it helps me to dip the ice cream earlier and put the separate scoops in a pan or dish that can be put in freezer. Then when time to fix the dessert it is easier to take out the pre-dipped ice cream.

Anytime Beef Tenderloin
Beef Tenderloin
Mushroom Sauce
Onion Cups With Peas
Cheesy Mashed Potatoes
Any Fruit Salad
German Chocolate Cheesecake

Roast Sirloin of Beef
Beef Rib Roast
Yorkshire Pudding
Marinated Asparagus Spears
Twice Baked Sweet Potatoes
Green Salad with Raspberry Dressing
Any Fruit in Season

I don't feel that I have ever perfected making Yorkshire Pudding. But since it is tradition to serve it, I do it occasionally. (But frankly I think it is overrated.)

Lasagna
Beef and Vegetable Lasagna
Green Salad
Garlic Toast
Peach Cobbler

I think this is the best and easiest lasagna that I have ever used. The recipe was printed in the Parade Magazine years ago.

Plank Meatloaf
Company Meatloaf
Duchess Potatoes
Baked Tomatoes Filled With Green Peas
Corn Muffins or Rolls
Strawberry Rhubarb Pie

This menu does not have to be served on a plank. It can as well be put together on a heat-proof platter. The Duchess Potatoes can line the platter as well as a plank, and be put under the broiler to brown.

Beef Wellington
Country Beef Wellington
Harvard Beets
Celery Casserole
Mixed Greens Salad
German Chocolate Cheesecake

This recipe is one of Emeril's. I watch his program occasionally on The Food Network. The Beef Wellington can be prepared early in the day and refrigerated until about one hour before serving. Let stand at room temperature for 30 minutes and then bake about 30 minutes.

Pot Roast
Deluxe Pot Roast with Vegetables
Baked Fruit Casserole
Hard Rolls or Corn Muffins
Rice Pudding

I don't know what could be better on a cold winter night than pot roast with root vegetables.

Swiss Steak For Company
Swiss Steak
White Rice
Broccoli Casserole
Any Fruit Salad
Corn Muffins or Hard Rolls
Custard Pie

John Orme Flanary and I used to exchange recipes a lot. This Swiss Steak recipe is from him.

Teriyaki Stir-Fry
Boneless Round Steak
Carrots
Celery
Onions
Rice
Spinach / Mandarin Orange Salad
Chocolate Cake

Beef Stew
Beef and Mushroom Stew
Spinach Casserole
Corn Salad
Corn Dodgers or French Garlic Toast
Ice Cream and Cookies

Chicken Dinner
Upper Crust Chicken
Mixed Squash and Tomato Casserole
Mixed Green Salad or Spinach Salad
Light Cheesecake with Berry Topping

Patty Shells Special
Chicken and Artichokes in Patty Shells
New Potatoes with Parsley
Lima Beans with Water Chestnuts
Applesauce Salad
Hard Rolls
Pumpkin Mousse

To me, a meal served in Patty Shells is always glamorous! At a luncheon, it is nice served on the plate. At a buffet dinner party, it is nice to let the guests serve themselves from the chafing dish with chicken and artichokes and the patty shells on a nearby heated platter.

Chicken with Ham
Baked Chicken Breast with Ham
New Potatoes Baked in Garlic Butter
Asparagus Vinaigrette
Cranberry Apple Mold
Baked Alaska

I suppose we all serve chicken in some form more than any other meat. This was one of Thomas' favorite chicken recipes. It is easy to prepare and good served with rice or potatoes.

All American
Fried Chicken and Gravy
Mashed Potatoes
Sweet and Sour Green Beans
Tomato/Cottage Cheese Salad
Hot Biscuits
Strawberry Shortcake

I guess if we were to pick one "All American" menu, this would be it! Everybody likes it.

Country Favorite
Oven Fried Chicken
Good Sweet Potatoes
Vegetable Vinaigrette Salad
Bread of Choice
Angel Food Cake, Strawberries with Whipped Cream

This recipe works well, for the chicken and the sweet potatoes can cook in the oven at same time.

Barbequed Chicken
Oven Barbecued Chicken
Corn on Cob
Three Bean Salad
Potato Salad
French Bread
Carrot Cake

Fancy Chicken
Stuffed Chicken Breasts
Baked New Potatoes in Garlic Butter
Green Beans
Tomato Aspic Salad
Key Lime Cheesecake

Tex-Mex
Tex-Mex Squash Chicken Casserole
Fried Green Tomatoes
Corn Salad
Flan

Country Ham Special
Fried Country Ham
Turnip Greens
Cheesy Mashed Potatoes
Corn Dodgers
Blackberry Cobbler

For those who like turnip greens this is, I guess, the number one dinner. This was another of Thomas' favorites. He was very fond of turnip greens and thought everyone should like them also. He gave some to his St. Bernard dog once and the dog, Brandy, turned the plate upside down and walked away! So Thomas, very disappointed, said that everybody (and every dog) has his own taste!

Buffet Style Dinner For 12
Pork Loin Roast with Apricot Orange Glaze
Salmon Mousse with Cucumber Sauce
Green Bean Bundles in Bacon
Baked New Potatoes in Garlic Butter
Mixed Vegetable Dish
Fresh Applesauce in Compote
French Bread in Flower Pots
Carrot Cake and Lime Cheesecake

This is the menu that I served for Julie and Keith Stout's joint birthday dinner on July 23, 2004. The guest list included their horseback riding friends. I think when a meal is served buffet style, it is particularly good to have two meat dishes and one more vegetable maybe than I would for a sit down dinner.

Pork Chops and Creamed Turnips
Baked Pork Chops
Creamed Turnips (My Way)
Green Peas and Carrots
Vinegar Slaw
Corn Dodgers
Banana Pudding

A lot of people say they don't like turnips any better than turnip greens - well please cook them my way! I think they are so good and maybe you will too!

Crown Pork Roast
Crown Pork Roast with Apple Raisin Stuffing
Twice Baked Potatoes
Brussels Sprouts with Almond Butter
Applesauce Salad
Commercial Hard Rolls
Pumpkin Chiffon Pie

Planked Salmon with spinach-stuffed tomato, green peas, Duchess Potatoes and Marguery Sauce

Thomas, Mary Lou, Perry Chipps, Ethel and Elizabeth Rogers

Dinner on a Plank
Salmon Steaks
Fruit Salad
Hot French Bread
Lemon Meringue Pie

I usually do this dinner with salmon; however fish, steak or meatloaf works well.

50

Seafood in Shells
Seafood Mornay
Marinated Asparagus
Mandarin Salad
Hot Rolls
General Robert E. Lee Orange Lemon Cake

Oven Poached Salmon
Whole Salmon Fillet
Twice Baked Potatoes
Broccoli with Horseradish Sauce
Tossed Mixed Green Salad
Hard Rolls
Lemon Chiffon Pie

Christmas 2000 – Thomas Tucker, J.D. Clopton, Alan Stout,
Doris Stout, Rev. Wayne Garvey, Julie Stout, Keith Stout,
(not visible, Erica Guess, Logan Stout, Katie Stout, Imogene
Stout James) and Mary Pogue (back to camera).

Christmas Dinner
Prime Rib Roast
Baked Ham
Mushroom Pie
Volcano Potatoes

Sautéed Brussels Sprouts with Almond Butter
Scalloped Oysters
Grapefruit-Avocado Salad
Relish Tray
Boiled Custard, Coconut Cake, Fruit Cake

This is the typical menu at our house when families get together for Christmas. It is served buffet style. The families furnish part of the food and I do most of the cooking, and a good time is had by all.

Thanksgiving Dinner
Turkey with Cornbread Dressing
Baked Ham
Volcano Potatoes
Sweet-Sour Green Beans
Candied Sweet Potatoes in Orange Shells
Corn Pudding
Scalloped Oysters
Cranberry Sauce
Relish Tray
Pumpkin Pie and Pecan Pie

This is the typical menu at our house when families get together. It is served buffet style. The families furnish part of the food and I cook it, and we all have a good time. This tradition started after World War II. New members come along and fill the chairs of those who have passed on.

Luncheon Menus

Turkey and Broccoli Mornay
Spiced Apple Ring
Congealed Strawberry-Pineapple Delight
Biscuits Supreme
Lemon Chiffon Pie

Chicken and Artichokes in Patty Shells
Grilled Tomato Florentine
Spinach Casserole
Lime Sherbet in Meringue

South Seas Chicken Salad
Asparagus Vinaigrette
Melon Balls with Orange Sauce
Banana Nut Bread

Shrimp and Crab Chanterelle
Tomato Stuffed with Cottage Cheese
Oatmeal Bread
French Silk Pie

Chicken Spinach/Mandarin Salad
Small Sandwiches, Assorted
Lemon Tarts

Ethel and Alex Yarbrough Pugh before morning bridal coffee

Party Menus

Morning Party For Alex Yarbrough
Mixed Fruit in Orange Baskets
Ham Salad and Beaten Biscuits
Chicken Salad Tarts
Thumb Print Cookies
Sour Cream Coffee Cake
Mixed Fruit Punch
Coffee

Christmas Coffee
Ham and Biscuit
Sausage Balls in Chafing Dish
Chicken Salad Tarts
Vegetable Tray with Dip
Assorted Cookies
Fruit Tray
Coffee Cake
Coffee and Tea

54

Chapter Four - Appetizers, Party Fare and Snacks

So whether you eat or drink or whatever you do,
do all to the glory of God.
1 Corinthians 10:31

As I've grown older, and I hope a bit wiser, I have changed my thinking about serving so many calories before a meal to whet the appetite. The obesity problem of the country, could have in part, stemmed from too much to whet the appetite to say nothing about change or lifestyle.

Most of the recipes in this section I would really call Party Fare. One can make a whole meal of them.

My dictionary defines appetizers as follows: a food or drink that stimulates the appetite and is usually served before a meal. Let's think seriously, do we need to stimulate our appetites?

Crab Appetizer Pizza

1 tube (8 ounce) crescent rolls
1 package (8ounce) cream cheese, softened
1 ½ cup coarsely chopped fresh spinach, divided
2 green onions, sliced thinly
1 ½ teaspoon minced fresh dill or ½ teaspoon dry dill weed
1 teaspoon lemon peel
½ teaspoon lemon juice
⅛ teaspoon pepper
¼ teaspoon salt
1 ½ cups chopped imitation crabmeat
¼ cup chopped ripe chives

Unroll crescent roll dough and place on a ungreased 12-inch pizza pan or cookie sheet. Flatten dough, sealing seams. Bake at 350 degrees for 8-10 minutes. Cool. In a small mixing bowl, beat cream cheese until smooth. Stir in 1 cup of spinach, onion dill, ½ teaspoon lemon peel, lemon juice and pepper and salt. Spread over crust. Top with crab, olives and the remaining spinach and lemon peel. Cut in bite size squares.

Sauerkraut Balls

1 pound can sauerkraut, rinsed and drained
1 (15-16 ounce) can corned beef, chopped
3 eggs, slightly beaten
½ cup finely chopped onion
2 cups fine breadcrumbs

Squeeze sauerkraut dry. Mix with corned beef, two of the eggs and chopped onion. When mixed well, form into walnut sized balls and freeze overnight. Remove from freezer and dip in beaten egg. Roll in breadcrumbs and deep fry at 350 degrees until golden.

Note: the balls may be put on a lightly greased cookie sheet and baked in a preheated 375-degree oven.

Cheese Puffs

3 cups grated sharp cheddar cheese
¾ cup soft butter
1 ½ cup flour
1 teaspoon paprika
Stuffed olives and/or cocktail onion

Mix cheese and butter, stir in flour and paprika. Mix well. Wrap about a teaspoon around each olive or onion. Freeze on a cookie sheet. Put in plastic bags after frozen. Take from freezer and bake 15 minutes on 400 degrees.

Cheese Wreath Spread

2 (8 ounce) packages cream cheese, softened
1 (8 ounce) package shredded cheddar
1 tablespoon each of chopped red pepper and green onions
2 teaspoons Worcestershire sauce
1 teaspoon lemon juice
Dash of ground red pepper

Beat cheeses together with electric mixer at medium speed until blended. Add remaining ingredients. Mix well. Refrigerate several hours. Place a drinking glass in center of serving plate or platter sprayed with Pam. Spoon the mixture to form a ring around the glass, just touching the glass. Smooth with a spatula. Remove glass and decorate top with parsley and red pepper. Serve with crackers or vegetable strips.

Artichoke Dip

2 (14 ounce) cans of artichoke hearts drained and chopped
1 cup mayonnaise
1 cup Parmesan cheese, grated
½ teaspoon garlic powder
Fresh ground black pepper

Mix all together and bake for 30 minutes at 250 degrees. Serve with breadsticks or crackers.

Peppery Spiced Nuts

2 tablespoons butter, melted
1 pound pecan halves
2 teaspoons Worcestershire sauce
½ teaspoon salt
⅛ teaspoon pepper

In skillet sauté nuts in butter until hot. Add other ingredients. Arrange nuts in a shallow pan and bake 20 minutes at 325 degrees.

Hot Spinach Dip

2 (10 ounce) packages frozen chopped spinach
¼ cup butter, melted
2 tablespoons chopped onion
3 tablespoons all-purpose flour
½ cup evaporated milk
1 (16 ounce) roll jalapeno cheese, softened
½ teaspoon pepper
¾ teaspoon celery salt
¾ teaspoon garlic salt
1 tablespoon Worcestershire sauce

Cook spinach according to package directions; drain well, reserving ½ cup liquid. Set aside. Combine butter, onion, and flour. Stir well and cook about 1 minute. Gradually add reserved spinach liquid and evaporated milk. Cook until slightly thickened, stirring constantly. Add cheese and seasonings to sauce, stirring until cheese is melted. Add spinach, mixing well. Serve with assorted crackers or vegetable sticks.

Spinach and Artichoke Dip

1 (16 ounce) carton light sour cream
1 (10 ounce) package Hidden Valley Ranch party dip mix
1 (14 ounce) can artichoke hearts, rinsed, drained and
    chopped
1 (10 ounce) frozen chopped spinach, thawed and drained
1 (2 ounce) jar diced pimento, drained
1 large round loaf bread
1 large loaf bread cut into cubes for dipping

Combine sour cream and party mix in medium bowl. Stir in artichokes, spinach and pimento. Cut slice off top of bread loaf. Hollow out center leaving one-inch shell. Reserve bread pieces for dipping. Spoon dip into bread shell for serving, warm or cold. To warm loaf, place in 400-degree oven for about 20 minutes. Serve with bread cubes and vegetables.

Navy Bean Dip

1 can white beans, drained
1 cup sour cream
1 tablespoon chopped green pepper
2 tablespoons chopped onion
¼ teaspoon garlic powder
¼ teaspoon cayenne pepper

Mash beans with fork. Add other ingredients. Taste and adjust seasonings. Heat in microwave. Serve with miniature Corn Dodgers or tortilla chips.

Note: see Corn Dodger recipe in bread section.

Taco Dip

1 package (8 ounce) cream cheese
2 cups (16 ounce) plain yogurt
1 package (1.25 ounce) dry taco seasoning
1 jar (8 ounce) taco sauce
½ head lettuce, shredded
2 tomatoes, chopped
½ cup black olives, sliced
¼ cup scallions or green onions
1 cup shredded cheddar cheese

Beat cream cheese until smooth. Stir in yogurt and taco seasoning. Chill. When ready to serve, spread yogurt mixture in bottom of bowl. Spread taco sauce and layer around edge the remainder of ingredients. Serve with corn chips.

Imogene's Meat Balls

2 pounds ground chuck
3 eggs
1 package Lipton Onion Soup Mix
1 cup breadcrumbs

Mix all together and make into about 70 meatballs. Put in a 13x9 pan.

In a pan, heat to boiling the following and pour over the meatballs.

1 bottle Heinz chili sauce
1 bottle water
½ cup brown sugar
1 cup pineapple chunks
1 can cranberry sauce

Bake uncovered 1 hour and then cover and cook one hour at 350 degrees. Serve in chaffing dish.

Stuffed Strawberries

2 dozen fresh strawberries, divided
1 (3 ounce) cream cheese, softened
3 tablespoons finely chopped pecans
2 tablespoons powdered sugar
1 teaspoon orange concentrate

Dice 3 or 4 strawberries – set aside. Cut a thin slice from stem end of each berry, making a base to stand on. Cut each berry into four wedges, starting on pointed ends and cutting almost but not through stem ends. Beat cream cheese until fluffy. Stir in diced strawberries and remainder of ingredients. Spoon or pipe about a teaspoon into each strawberry.

Note: Make stuffing and prepare berries a day ahead, but do not fill strawberries more than 4 hours before serving.

Pecan Raisin Mini Tarts

1 cup sugar
¼ cup butter or margarine, melted
2 large eggs, beaten
1 tablespoon white vinegar
½ teaspoon cinnamon
½ teaspoon nutmeg
1 cup golden raisins
1 cup chopped pecans, toasted
3 (2.1 ounce) packages frozen mini pylo tart shells

Stir together first six ingredients. Stir in raisins and pecans. Spoon filling into frozen tart shells and place on a baking sheet. Bake at 325 degrees for 20-25 minutes. Cool and garnish if desired.

Creamy Pecan Fudge

3 (12 ounce) packages semi sweet chocolate morsels
1 (7 ounce) jar marshmallow cream
1 cup butter or margarine
4 ½ cups sugar
1 (13 ounce) can evaporated milk
3 cups chopped pecans, or more

Combine chocolate morsels, marshmallow cream, and butter in a large bowl. Combine sugar and evaporated milk in saucepan. Bring to boil, then reduce heat and cook over low heat 9 minutes, stirring constantly. Pour over chocolate morsel mixture; stirring until chocolate melts and mixture is smooth. Add pecans. Spread mixture in a lightly greased 15x10 inch jelly roll pan. Chill until firm, then cut into squares.

Strawberries Dipped in White Chocolate

2 pints fresh berries
6 ounces white chocolate or white flavored chocolate
   baking bar, grated

Rinse berries and dry thoroughly. Set berries aside. Place chocolate in top of double boiler. Bring water to a boil. Reduce heat to low and cook until chocolate melts. Hold berry by stem and dip into melted chocolate. Place on a wire rack sprayed with cooking spray and chill until firm. Should be served within 6-8 hours.

Hot Mushroom Turnovers

1 (8 ounce) package cream cheese, softened
½ cup butter or margarine, softened
1 ½ cups all-purpose flour
¼ pound fresh mushrooms, diced
1 medium onion, minced
1 ½ tablespoon butter or margarine, melted
2 tablespoons sour cream
1 tablespoon flour
½ teaspoon salt
⅛ teaspoon thyme
1 egg, beaten

Make dough with first three items. Shape into a ball, and cover with plastic. Sauté mushrooms and onions in 1 ½ tablespoons butter in heavy skillet over low heat. Remove from heat and stir in sour cream and next three ingredients; set aside. Roll pastry to ⅛ inch on lightly floured board. Cut with three-inch cutter. Place ½ teaspoon of mixture in center of each circle. Brush edges with egg and fold dough in half, pressing to seal edges. Crimp edges with fork and also prick tops. Brush with egg. Place 1 inch apart on ungreased cookie sheet. Bake at 450 degrees for 12 minutes or until golden.

Note: Turnovers may be frozen either baked or unbaked. Follow usual procedure.

Stuffed New Potatoes

20 red – skinned new potatoes, scrubbed
2 medium stalks celery, chopped small
1 carrot diced fine
1 small onion, diced fine
2 hard-boiled eggs coarsely chopped
2 tablespoons green relish
2 tablespoons fresh dill (if available), chopped
1 tablespoon parsley, chopped
¾ teaspoon fresh ground pepper
½ teaspoon salt
⅛ teaspoon sugar
1 cup mayonnaise
1 cup sour cream

Drop potatoes into large pot of boiling water and cook about 12 minutes, until tender. Drain. When potatoes are cool, cut in half. Cut a tiny slice off bottom of each so they will set upright. With a small scoop, scoop out center of each potato half, leaving a strong shell about ¼ inch. Place potato centers in a bowl, and reserve the shells. Gently toss potato centers with next 10 ingredients. Mix mayonnaise and sour cream together, and then gently fold into the potato salad. Taste and adjust seasoning if needed. With small spoon, mound salad into shells. Garnish with dill and paprika at serving time.

Artichoke Stuffed Mushrooms

1 ½ pounds large fresh mushrooms
¼ cup chopped onion
2 garlic cloves pressed or minced
1 tablespoon olive oil
¼ cup white cooking wine
¼ cup soft breadcrumbs
1 (14 ounce) can artichoke hearts, drained and chopped
3 green onions, chopped
½ cup grated Parmesan cheese
½ cup mayonnaise
¼ teaspoon each of salt, pepper and sugar

Rinse and dry mushrooms. Remove stems and chop, reserve caps. Sauté mushrooms, stems, onion, garlic in hot oil over medium heat for 5 minutes or until onion is tender. Add wine and cook 2 minutes. Stir in breadcrumbs. Remove from heat and let cool. Combine onion mixture, artichoke and next 6 ingredients. Taste for seasonings. Spoon 1 teaspoon into each mushroom cap. Place on slightly greased rack in shallow roasting pan. Bake at 350 degree for 12 to 15 minutes.

Crabmeat Tarts

1 can crabmeat, drained
1 tablespoon lemon juice
1 cup celery, finely chopped
½ cup green onions, finely chopped
½ cup sharp cheddar cheese
½ teaspoon Tabasco sauce
1 pinch salt

Mix all together and bake in Cream Cheese Pastry.

Cream Cheese Pastry

1 (3 ounce) package cream cheese
1 cup grated cheddar cheese
1 cup flour

Mix all together. Form pastry into small balls. Put one ball in each mini muffin tin and form into a crust. Fill with crabmeat mixture and bake about 30 minutes at 325 degrees.

Chicken Salad Tarts

2 ¼ cups all-purpose flour
½ teaspoon salt
¼ teaspoon sugar
½ cup shortening
¼ cup butter
½ -⅔ cup milk
4 cups finely chopped cooked chicken
2 stalks celery, finely chopped
½ cup slivered almonds, toasted
⅔ cup mayonnaise
2 tablespoons steak sauce
½ teaspoon curry powder
½ teaspoon seasoning salt and garlic salt
Pimento bits

Make crust of first 6 ingredients. Shape dough into about 60 balls. Place in ungreased muffin tins and shape each ball into a shell. Bake at 400 degrees for 12 minutes. Combine rest of ingredients, cover and chill at least 1 hour. Spoon into cooled tart shells. Garnish with pimento and small sprig of parsley.

Note: May substitute bought pie crust or make the cream cheese tart crust.

Filled Flower Pots

Unsliced bread – homemade
2 cans (6 ounces) flaked crabmeat
1 cup celery, diced
½ cup bell pepper, diced
½ teaspoon salt
Dash fresh ground pepper
2 tablespoons lemon juice
⅔ cup mayonnaise
Sprigs of parsley

Cut bread into one-inch slices. Freeze. Cut circles in frozen slices with a one- inch round cutter. Scoop out centers leaving ¼ inch thick. Blend all ingredients together, except parsley, and then chill. Toast pots in oven. Fill with crabmeat mixture and garnish with parsley.

Asparagus Roll-ups

24 asparagus spears
1 (8 ounce) package cream cheese softened
1 (4 ounce) package crumbled blue cheese
2 tablespoons mayonnaise
1 tablespoon chopped fresh chives
12 bread slices, trimmed
12 thin slices deli ham
¼ cup butter or margarine, melted
Paprika

Snap off ends of asparagus and remove scales from stalks. Arrange asparagus in a steamer basket over boiling water. Cover and steam 4-6 minutes. Remove and cool on paper towels. Stir together cream cheese and next 3 ingredients. Roll each bread slice with rolling pin to flatten. Spread one side of each slice with cream cheese mixture. Top each with ham slice. Place two asparagus spears, tips pointed to opposite ends, on one end of bread slices, roll up, and place seam side down on a greased baking sheet. Brush with melted butter and sprinkle with paprika. Bake at 400 degrees for 12 minutes. Serve immediately. Unbaked roll-ups can be frozen. Thaw in refrigerator and bake as directed.

Christmas Relish Tree

2 bunches curly endive
Florist picks or heavy toothpicks
1 plastic foam cone with nine-inch base, about 1 foot tall
1 carton cherry tomatoes
1 zucchini, sliced thinly
½ head cauliflower, separated into flowerettes
4 carrots, cut into 2 inch sticks
Radish roses

Wash and separate endive, and remove tough end of each leaf. Begin to form the tree by attaching leaves to the bottom of the cone with florist picks and move upward, completely covering cone with endive. Attach vegetables to endive-covered cone with wooden picks. Do this to look like decorations on a Christmas tree. Place tree on tray. Serve with any dip.

Ranch Oyster Crackers

1 (1 ounce) package Hidden Valley original ranch dressing
¼ cup oil
1 (12 ounce) package plain oyster cracker. Stir to coat.

Bake 15-20 minutes at 250 degrees. Stir after 10 minutes.

Toasted Pecans or Almonds

½ cup butter or margarine, melted
3 cups nuts
Salt to taste

Pour butter over pecans or almonds, stirring to coat well. Arrange pecans or almonds in a single layer on a baking sheet, sprinkle with salt. Bake at 275 degrees about 1 hour. Stir occasionally.

Praline Pecan Crunch

1 (16 ounce) box Quaker Oat Squares cereal (8 cups)
2 cups pecan pieces
½ cup light corn syrup
½ cup firmly packed brown sugar
¼ cup margarine
1 teaspoon vanilla
½ teaspoon baking soda

Heat oven to 250 degrees. Combine cereal and pecans in a 13x9 pan, set aside. Combine corn syrup, brown sugar and margarine in a 2-cup microwave safe bowl. Microwave on high 1 ½ minutes, stir, microwave on high ½ to 1 minute more or until it boils. Stir in vanilla and baking soda and pour over cereal mixture to coat evenly. Bake 1 hour, stirring every 20 minutes. Spread on baking sheet to cool. Break into pieces.

Makes 10 cups

Chapter Five - Salads, Soups and Sandwiches

When I was growing up, we did not have salads as we know them today in this rural area.

In the spring, we had wilted lettuce, mustard and tender wild greens! We made salad using wilted lettuce, bacon drippings, sugar, green onions and vinegar. Later in the season, sliced tomatoes, green peppers, green onions and cucumbers were available on every family's table if they raised a garden. As I remember it, they were put on different plates, for one child liked one and not the other; if it touched what they did not like, they would not eat it. This was also the time when lots of canning went on to prepare for the following winter.

The big assortments of commercial salad dressings as we know them today were not on the market until about the last half of the 20th century.

Fresh fruits and vegetables were just not available out of season. During the local harvest season is when the canning took place, canning tomatoes, peaches, apples, and making pickles, jellies and preserves for the winter.

My first real remembrance of eating an orange and drinking orange juice was in 8th grade, when I was 12 years old. Our teacher Mabel Minner gave us students an orange that she had garnished with a stick of peppermint candy stuck in its core. You sucked the orange juice through the peppermint.

When you walk into the grocery store now you should thank our Master that we have all this bounty of good healthy fruit and vegetables, realizing that progress has come a long way for this generation to enjoy the salads today!

And a word about Chicken Salad: Someone remarked to me the other day that they did not think chicken salad was as good as it used to be!

Chicken salad is almost a staple on our menus during the summer season. I make it frequently, but I do not make it by the same recipe. This gives my extended family something different to comment on and compliment. I told this person, and I might suggest to you, to try a different recipe sometime! Who knows, you might like it!

Chicken Spinach / Mandarin Salad

6 skinned, boneless chicken breasts
1 (3 ounce) package Ramen noodles, toasted
8 cups greens, spinach and tender lettuce
2 bunches green onions
1-2 cups diced celery
½ cup toasted slivered almonds
2 (11 ounce) cans mandarin oranges

Mix greens, celery, and onions. Chill. Marinate the chicken breasts in teriyaki sauce overnight. Then broil in oven or grill, whichever is easiest. Cut into strips.

The Dressing: Put all ingredients in a blender
1 cup olive oil
½ cup sugar
¼ cup white wine vinegar
¼ cup rice vinegar
¼ cup honey
2 tablespoons poppy seeds
1 tablespoon prepared mustard
½ teaspoon salt
Mix and taste. Adjust seasonings as desired.

To assemble:

Put part of dressing over greens and mix. Put approximately one cup greens on 8 plates and divide the oranges, noodles and almonds. Then arrange the chicken strips and drizzle more dressing over it.

8 Servings

Applesauce Salad

¾ cup red hots
4 ½ cups boiling water
9 ounces (three small packages) lemon Jell-O
3 ½ cups applesauce
A pinch of salt and pepper

Dissolve red hots in boiling water. Add Jell-O and stir, and then salt and pepper. Chill a short time, then stir in applesauce. Spray 12 individual molds with cooking spray and pour salad in. Let them set-up in refrigerator a few hours or overnight. Remove from mold and place on lettuce leaf and top with mayonnaise.

Bavarian Kraut Salad

1 can Bavarian kraut, drained
½ cup chopped onion
½ cup chopped green pepper
½ cup chopped celery
1 cup sugar
½ cup vinegar

Mix first 4 ingredients. Combine sugar and vinegar and heat to boil. Pour over chopped vegetables and Kraut. Chill before serving. This tart taste is particularly appealing when the entrée is of mild flavor.

California Chicken Salad

3 cups cubed cooked chicken
1 ½ cups red seedless grapes
1 cup sliced celery
½ cup broken walnuts
⅓ cup sliced green onions
¾ cup mayonnaise
½ teaspoon ground ginger

In a large bowl, combine mayonnaise and ginger. Stir in chicken, grapes, celery, walnuts and green onions. Cover to blend flavors before serving.

Fruited Chicken Salad

4 cups chopped cooked chicken
1 cup diced celery
2 tablespoons minced sweet red onion, or green onions
1 (15 ounce) can chunk pineapple, drained
1 cup green seedless grapes, halved
¾ cup mayonnaise
¼ cup whipping cream or sour cream
1 teaspoon sugar
½ teaspoon salt
¼ teaspoon white pepper
1 tablespoon lemon juice
½ cup toasted, slivered almonds

In a large bowl combine first five ingredients. In a small bowl mix next 6 ingredients; add to first mixture. Chill at least 1 hour. Serve on lettuce cup and sprinkle with toasted almonds and paprika.

When I have plenty of time, I like to cook the chicken breasts in just enough water to barely cover, including some celery leaves, a slice of onion, peppercorns and some salt. Cook until tender. Strain broth and save for soup or a casserole. If I'm in a hurry I cook

72

the chicken breasts in the microwave, which will take less than five minutes if the chicken breasts are not frozen.

Hot Chicken Salad # 1

4 cups cooked, chopped chicken
4 tablespoons chopped pimento
1 can sliced water chestnuts, drained
1 cup mayonnaise
1 cup finely chopped celery
1 can cream of chicken soup, undiluted
½ teaspoon white pepper
Pinch sugar

Mix all ingredients, taste for seasonings, put in casserole and top with crushed potato chips and heat until bubbly in a 350 degree oven.

This is a recipe used by the churchwomen all over the district. It is easy, and it is good!

Hot Chicken Salad # 2

3 cups cooked chicken, chopped
2 cups celery, chopped fine
2 teaspoons diced pimento
1 teaspoon salt
¼ teaspoon pepper
¼ cup Swiss cheese, grated
¾ cups mayonnaise

Mix all ingredients together. Bake 30 minutes at 350 degrees. Cover top with crushed potato chips the last 5 minutes of baking.

Mediterranean Chicken Salad

1 pound chicken breast halves
3 tablespoons red wine vinegar
1 clove garlic crushed
½ teaspoon oregano
¼ teaspoon freshly ground pepper
¾ cup olive oil
1 pound corkscrew spiral noodles
1 head broccoli flowerettes
5 ounces pepperoni, diced
2 tablespoons capers
¼ pound feta cheese, crumbled
Salt to taste

Cook chicken in simmering water for 20 minutes. When cool, remove skin and bones and dice. Combine vinegar, garlic, oregano, pepper and olive oil in blender or glass jar with tight lid. Shake well. Cook spiral noodles according to package directions. Drain and rinse well with cold water. Drain again. Toss with dressing in large bowl. Cook broccoli until barely tender and bright green. Rinse under cold water and drain well. Combine all ingredients with noodles. Salt to taste and chill before serving.

Serves 8-10

South Seas Chicken Salad

2 quarts cooked, chopped chicken
1 (8 ½ ounce) can water chestnuts, sliced
2 pounds seedless green grapes, halved
2 cups diced celery
2 tablespoons soy sauce
2 cups toasted almonds
3 cups mayonnaise
1 tablespoon curry powder

Mix chicken, water chestnuts, grapes, celery and almonds. Combine mayonnaise, curry powder and soy sauce. Fold into chicken mixture. It is nice to serve it on a tomato or cantaloupe slice.

This recipe is a popular version of the many chicken salad recipes used in our community. Susan Yargrough, a cook of the month, recently shared this recipe in our local paper, The Crittenden Press. She very kindly gave credit to some of the older ladies of another era who encouraged her through the years.

Serve 12-14

Vegetable Chicken Salad

4 cups cooked chicken, chopped
4 hard boiled eggs, chopped
1 ½ cups frozen green peas, cooked to tender in microwave
½ cup chopped celery
½ cup sweet onion, chopped
¼ cup sweet pickle relish
½ teaspoon curry powder
½ teaspoon salt
½ teaspoon fresh ground pepper
Pinch of sugar
1 cup mayonnaise
½ cup sour cream

Mix mayonnaise, sour cream, sugar, pepper, salt and curry. Mix chicken, peas, celery, onion, relish and eggs, lightly. Add the dressing mixture, stir lightly and taste for seasonings. Serve on lettuce leaf for individual serving and sprinkle with paprika and add a sprig of parsley, if available.

This was the chicken salad that my mother used to make, and I learned from her to make it and I am very fond of it!

10-12 servings

Marinated Corn Salad

2 (11 ounce) cans whole kernel corn, drained
1 medium onion, chopped
1 small sweet red pepper, chopped
1 small green pepper, chopped
¼ cup minced fresh parsley
¼ cup cider vinegar
2 tablespoons vegetable oil
1 teaspoon sugar
½ teaspoon salt
½ teaspoon pepper
Curly lettuce leaves (optional)

Combine corn, onion, sweet red pepper, green pepper, and parsley in a medium bowl. Stir well. Combine vinegar, oil, salt, and pepper. Stir well. Pour vinegar mixture over corn mixture. Toss gently to combine. Cover and chill at least 8 hours. Serve in a lettuce-lined salad bowl, if desired.

8 servings

Cranberry-Apple Mold

1 (3 ounce) package raspberry-flavored gelatin
¼ cup boiling water
1 (8 ounce) can crushed pineapple, drained
1 (16 ounce) can whole berry cranberry sauce
1 red delicious apple, unpeeled and coarsely chopped
1 tablespoon grated orange rind
⅛ teaspoon salt
⅛ teaspoon ground cinnamon
Dash of ground cloves
Lettuce leaves

Dissolve raspberry flavored gelatin in boiling water, and let cool. Stir in next 7 ingredients and spoon into a lightly oiled 4-cup mold. Cover and chill until firm. Remove from mold on lettuce-lined platter and garnish with orange strips.

Serves 8

Cranberry Mouse

1 (20 ounce) can crushed pineapple
1 (6 ounce) package strawberry gelatin
1 cup water
1 (1 pound) can whole cranberry sauce
3 tablespoons lemon juice
1 teaspoon lemon peel
¼ teaspoon nutmeg
Few grains black pepper
2 cups dairy sour cream
½ cup chopped pecans

Drain pineapple well, reserving all juice. Add juice to gelatin in a 2 quart pan. Stir in water. Heat to boiling, stirring to dissolve gelatin. Remove from heat. Blend in cranberry sauce. Add lemon juice, peel and nutmeg. Chill until mixture thickens slightly. Blend in sour cream. Fold in pineapple and pecans. Pour into 2 quart mold. Chill until firm. Remove from mold onto serving plate.

Serves 8

5 Cup Salad

1 cup orange sections
1 cup diced pineapple
1 cup shredded coconut
1 cup small marshmallows
1 cup broken pecans

Combine all ingredients. Cream ¼ cup cream cheese and blend in ½ cup sour cream for a dressing for the salad.

Frozen Fruit Salad

1 (8 ounce) cream cheese
1 (8 ounce) sour cream
2 tablespoons lemon juice
¾ cup white sugar
½ cup maraschino cherries, sliced
½ cup chopped pecans
1 (8 ounce) can crushed pineapple
3 bananas, sliced
⅛ teaspoon salt
1 can fruit cocktail, drained

Blend softened cheese, lemon juice and sugar. Stir in rest of ingredients and pour into a mold or 8x11 inch dish. Freeze.

Lime Mist

2 (3 ounce) packages lime gelatin
2 cups applesauce
1 cup chopped celery
¼ cup chopped nuts
¼ cup well drained, chopped maraschino cherries
2 cups lemon-lime carbonated beverage
1 cup Carnation milk
2 tablespoons lemon juice
Green cake color

Combine lime gelatin and applesauce in saucepan and heat over low heat until gelatin dissolves. Cool. Stir celery, nuts, maraschino cherries and lemon-lime beverage. Chill until syrupy. Chill milk until very cold; whip until stiff. Add lemon juice and whip until very stiff. Fold into gelatin mixture. Add a few drops green food color. Spoon into a 2 quart mold. Chill until firm.

Mandarin Orange Salad

1 (8 ounce) can crushed pineapple, not drained
1 (10 ounce) can mandarin oranges, not drained
3 (3 ounce) packages orange flavored gelatin
1 cup boiling water
1 pint orange sherbet
1 cup diced or miniature marshmallows
1 cup whipping cream, or 1 cup frozen whipped topping
thawed (shredded coconut, maraschino cherries or nuts,
optional)

Drain juices from pineapple and oranges; combine in a measuring cup to equal 1 cup liquid. Set juice aside. Dissolve gelatin in boiling water. Add fruit juices and stir well. Stir sherbet into hot gelatin and add fruit and marshmallows. Fold in whipped cream. Pour mixture into a 9x13 dish. Chill until set.

Mixed Fruit and Melon Salad

- serve in orange shells –

6 oranges cut in half and sections removed, save shells
1 cup assorted melon balls, or what's available
1 cup green grapes, halved
1 cup red grapes, halved
1 cup strawberries, halved or quartered to make about the
size of others
1 cup orange sections from the six oranges

Put all together in large bowl and pour sauce over to marinate for 30 minutes before serving. Fill each orange half shell and put on serving tray. If in season stick a sprig of mint in top.

This makes an attractive display on the table for a morning party, or an afternoon tea.

Sauce:

> Rind of 1 orange, grated
> Rind of 1 lemon, grated
> Juice of 1 lemon
> 1 ½ cups sugar

Cook in top of double boiler until thick and clear. Chill.

Overnight Salad

In a large straight sided bowl, layer these ingredients in order listed. The bowl should be one to take to the table at serving time.

> Head of lettuce torn into bite size pieces
> 1 cup diced celery
> 1 purple onion sliced; rings separated and spread over celery
> 1 (10 ounce) package frozen peas, thawed
> 1 cup mayonnaise, spread over top of peas
> ⅓ cup sugar sprinkled over mayonnaise
> 6 slices bacon, cooked crisp and crumbled over top (at serving time)

Put tight fitting lid on bowl or cover with double thick plastic wrap.

Tomato-Artichoke Aspic

> 4 envelopes unflavored gelatin
> ¾ cup cold water
> 5 cups vegetable cocktail juice
> 1 tablespoon lemon juice
> 1 teaspoon Worcestershire sauce
> ¼ teaspoon hot sauce

¼ teaspoon white pepper
1 (14 ounce) can artichoke hearts, drained and chopped
    coarsely
¼ cup minced parsley
5 carrots, finely chopped
Lettuce leaves
Paprika

Sprinkle gelatin over cold water and let stand 5 minutes. Bring vegetable cocktail juice to a boil. Add gelatin and cook over medium heat until gelatin dissolves, stirring constantly. Stir in lemon juice, Worcestershire sauce, hot sauce and pepper. Chill until consistency of unbeaten egg whites. Fold in next 5 ingredients; spoon into a lightly oiled 9-cup mold. Cover and chill until firm. To serve, remove from mold on a lettuce-lined plate. Garnish with paprika.

Apricot Salad

2 (3 ounce) packages lemon Jell-O
1 (3 ounce) package apricot Jell-O
2 cans apricot nectar
1 large can crushed pineapple, drained
1 or 2 cans mandarin oranges, cut up

Drain pineapple and oranges and save juices; mix with apricot nectar and enough water to make a total liquid of 5 ¾ cups. Heat part of the liquid and dissolve Jell-O in it. Add balance of liquid. When cool, add drained fruit and put in a 13x9 dish, which has been sprayed with vegetable spray.

Potato Salad

5 to 6 cups potatoes, boiled, peeled and diced (about 3
    pounds)
¼ green pepper, chopped
6 hard-boiled eggs, chopped

1 sweet onion, chopped
¼ cup sweet pickle relish
¾ cup mayonnaise
¾ cup salad dressing
1 teaspoon salt
¼ teaspoon white mustard seeds
¼ teaspoon celery seeds
¼ teaspoon sugar

Salt the diced potatoes while they are still warm, then add the mustard seed and the celery seed and sugar. Stir gently and then add other ingredients, letting the chopped eggs be the last item added. Taste and adjust seasonings.

This is the potato salad that I usually take to potluck meals. When I change and take something else, someone is sure to ask me, "Where's that potato salad?"

Tomato Surprise Salad

1 (1 pound) can stewed tomatoes
1 (3 ounce) package lemon Jell-O
¼ teaspoon salt
1 tablespoon vinegar
1 teaspoon sugar

Pour tomatoes in pan and save the can to mold in. Bring tomatoes to a boil. Reduce heat and simmer for 2 minutes. Add Jell-O, salt, vinegar and sugar and stir until dissolved. Pour back into the can. Chill until firm. Puncture bottom of can. Dip in warm water and remove from mold. Slice into six servings.

This is a delicious salad and so easy to make. I also mold it in individual molds if I am wanting to use it for individual salads. Serve it on lettuce leaf and top with mayonnaise and sour cream mixed together if desired. You can also use the stewed tomatoes with vegetables, instead of plain tomatoes, for a change.

Taco Salad

1 pound ground beef
1 (1 ¼ ounce) package taco seasoning mix
1 can (16 ounce) refried beans
1 jar (16 ounce) taco sauce
Approx. 6 cups lettuce, torn in bite size pieces
½ cup ripe olives
½ cup chopped onion
1 large tomato, chopped
1 ripe avocado, diced
1 cup shredded cheese
1 cup taco shells, broken, or corn chips

To prepare ground beef: cook in skillet until no longer pink, drain, add seasoning packet and continue as per its directions. Add refried beans and ½ of the taco sauce. In a large bowl, arrange ½ of the lettuce. Add the beef mixture. Top with remaining lettuce, olives, onion, tomato, avocado, cheese and chips. Serve with remaining sauce and a doll-up of sour cream.

Waldorf Salad

1 ½ cups diced, unpeeled red apples
1 tablespoon lemon juice
1 cup celery, diced
½ cup mayonnaise
1 cup walnuts
Crisp lettuce leaves

Mix all ingredients together and serve on the lettuce leaves on salad plates.

Did you ever wonder about the origin of a recipe? Waldorf Salad was created by the maitre d at the opening of the Waldorf Hotel on Fifth Avenue in New York City in March 1893, for the first public charity ball in history. It was a benefit given by Mrs. William K. Vanderbilt for St. Mary's Free Hospital for Children.

In 1893, the Waldorf Salad was a revolutionary combination of foods because people didn't eat fruit in salads as they do now. This started the fruit salad vogue. No written recipe exists of the original recipe. Culinary creations are usually made at the spur of the moment. It is believed that the first, or original salad, did not have nuts, which of course are an integral part of this salad.

Fresh Vegetable Marinade

4 stalks fresh broccoli
8 large fresh mushrooms, sliced
1 medium size green pepper, chopped
3 stalks celery, chopped
1 small head cauliflower, broken into flowerettes
1 cup sugar
2 teaspoons dry mustard
1 teaspoon salt
½ cup vinegar
½ cups vegetable oil
1 small onion, chopped or grated
1 tablespoon poppy seeds
1 teaspoon celery seeds

Remove flowerettes from broccoli and cut into bite-sized pieces. Combine flowerettes, mushrooms, pepper, celery and cauliflower; toss lightly. Combine remaining ingredients. Mix well and pour over the vegetables. Chill at least 3 hours. Yield 10 to 12 servings.

Wilted Lettuce Salad

Fresh, young lettuce leaves, torn to bite size, optional
2 hard boiled eggs, chopped coarsely
3-4 green onions, optional
4-6 slices bacon, fried crisp and crumbled

Dressing:

In the bacon drippings in the skillet, add ¼ cup sugar, ¼ cup water and ¼ cup vinegar and salt and fresh ground pepper to taste. Let it boil up and taste. Adjust seasonings if needed. Pour over the tossed salad.

This dressing works well over fresh mixed greens.

Poppy Seed Dressing No. 1

3 tablespoons chopped onion
⅔ cup apple cider vinegar
1 ½ cups sugar
2 teaspoons dry mustard
2 teaspoons salt
2 cups salad oil
3 tablespoons poppy seeds

Using a blender or food processor, mix onion and vinegar, blending until onion is finely chopped. Add sugar, mustard, salt and a pinch of pepper. Blend again. With machine running, add oil slowly until the mixture thickens. Stir in poppy seeds.

Poppy Dressing No. 2

1 cup olive oil
½ cup sugar
¼ cup white wine vinegar
¼ cup rice vinegar
¼ cup honey
2 tablespoons poppy seeds
1 tablespoon prepared mustard
½ teaspoon salt
¼ teaspoon freshly ground pepper

Put all the ingredients except the poppy seed and oil in the blender and blend well. Slowly add the oil. Stir in poppy seeds.

Raspberry Vinaigrette

1 tablespoon raspberry preserves
1 ½ teaspoon salt
1 ½ teaspoon fresh ground black pepper
¼ teaspoon minced garlic
¼ cup raspberry vinegar
1 ½ cup good oil

Combine all ingredients except oil in blender. Blend well. Slowly add oil. Especially good on fresh, green salad.

Soups

Artichoke Soup

(serve hot or cold)

1 can chicken broth
1 (8 ounce) package cream cheese
2 small cans petite artichokes hearts
1 can green chili peppers
Pinch of sugar

Blend all together, taste and adjust seasoning. Serve and garnish with a sour cream dollup.

Baked Potato Soup

⅔ cup butter of margarine
⅔ cup flour
7 cups milk

4 large baking potatoes, baked, cooled, peeled and diced
4 green onions, sliced
12 strips bacon, cooked and crumbled
1 ¼ cup shredded cheddar cheese
1 cup sour cream
¾ teaspoon salt
½ teaspoon white pepper
Pinch of sugar

In a large kettle, melt butter. Stir in flour. Heat and stir until a smooth roux. Gradually add milk, stirring constantly until thickened. Add potatoes and onions. Bring to a boil, stirring constantly. Reduce heat; simmer for 10 minutes. Add remaining ingredients. Stir until cheese melts.

Chicken Vegetable Chili

6-8 chicken breast halves, boned and skinned
2 onions, chopped
1 green pepper, chopped
1 yellow pepper, chopped
4 cloves garlic, pressed
2-4 tablespoons oil
4 (14 ½ ounce) cans stewed tomatoes, chopped
2 (15 ounce) cans white beans, drained
1 ½ cup Picante sauce
2 teaspoons chili powder
2 teaspoons cumin
1 teaspoon salt
¼ teaspoon sugar
For toppings: shredded cheddar, chopped onion, sour
    cream, diced avocado

12-14 servings

Cut chicken into one-inch pieces. Cook chicken and next three ingredients in hot oil in pot until slightly browned. Add tomatoes and next 6 ingredients. Cover and bring to a boil. Reduce heat and cook 20 minutes. Taste for seasonings.

Chunky Chicken Rice Soup

6 ounces boneless, skinless chicken breasts, cubed (about 1 cup)
1 teaspoon oil
2 (13 ¾ ounce) cans chicken broth
1 cup water
1 (10 ounce) package frozen mixed vegetables, thawed
½ teaspoon poultry seasoning
¼ teaspoon fresh ground pepper
1 cup minute rice
1 tablespoon chopped parsley

Cook and stir chicken in hot oil in saucepan until browned. Add broth, water, vegetables and seasonings. Bring to a boil, reduce heat to low, cover and simmer for 5 minutes. Stir in rice and parsley. Let stand 5 minutes.

Corn Chowder

1 large potato, peeled and diced
1 cup water
1 small onion, sliced
½ teaspoon salt
Pinch of sugar
2 tablespoons melted margarine
2 tablespoons flour
3 cups corn, fresh or canned
1 cup water
2 cups milk

Salt and pepper to taste
Cheese croutons

Combine potato, 1 cup water, onion and salt in saucepan. Bring to boil. Lower heat. Cover and simmer until vegetables are crisp tender, about 10 minutes. Transfer potato mixture to blender or food processor. Add melted butter or margarine and flour. Blend until smooth. Return potato puree to saucepan. Bring to boil. Lower heat and stir in corn, 1 cup water and milk. Add salt and pepper to taste. Serve at once and garnish with cheese croutons.

Corn and Okra Creole

1 cup chopped green pepper
½ cup chopped onion
2 tablespoons butter or margarine, melted
1 ½ cups white corn cut from cob, about three ears
½ cup water
2 medium tomatoes, peeled, seeded and chopped
1 ½ tablespoons tomato paste
¼ teaspoon dry thyme
¼ teaspoon paprika
½ teaspoon salt
¼ teaspoon pepper
1 ½ cups sliced okra

Sauté green pepper and onion in butter in a large skillet until crisp tender. Add corn and water. Cover and cook over medium heat 10 minutes, stirring occasionally. Add tomatoes and remaining ingredients except okra. Cover and simmer 10 minutes, stirring occasionally. Add okra. Cover and simmer 5 to 7 minutes or until okra is done.

Cream Leek Soup

¼ cup unsalted butter
2 pounds leeks (white and light green) coarsely chopped
2 large celery stalks, chopped
1 small russet potato, peeled and coarsely chopped
6 cups beef stock
¼ cup minced fresh parsley
½ teaspoon freshly grated nutmeg
½ cup (or more) whipping cream
Salt and freshly ground pepper

Melt butter in heavy large saucepan over low heat. Add leeks, onions, celery and potato and cook until tender and golden brown, stirring occasionally, about 20 minutes. Add stock, parsley and nutmeg. Cover and simmer 1 hour or until thickened. Puree soup in batches in blender or food processor. Return to saucepan. Mix in ½ cup cream. Stir until heated through. Season with salt and pepper. Ladle soup into bowls and top each with cream and nutmeg.

Cucumber Soup

3 to 4 large cucumbers
Salt
⅓ cup chopped green onions with tender tops
¼ teaspoon sugar
¼ teaspoon wine vinegar
Fresh or dry dill leaves
White pepper
½ cup watercress
½ cup sour cream
Thin cucumber slices for garnish

Peel and halve the cucumbers. Scrape out the seeds and juice (a teaspoon is the easiest way for removing seeds out of the cucumbers. Seeds and juice go into a strainer over a bowl). Sprinkle with ½ teaspoon salt and let drain. Process with steel blade. Drop in the chopped onions, cucumbers, sugar, vinegar, about ¼ teaspoon dill, watercress and the juices from the cucumber seeds. Whip in ¼ cup sour cream. Taste and correct seasoning if needed. Refrigerate an hour or more to blend flavors. Add ¼ cup sour cream, stir and taste again. Pour into bowls and decorate top with thin slices of cucumber.

Serve 6

Crock Pot Chicken Stew

6 boneless, skinless chicken thighs
2 large sweet potatoes, peeled and cut in chunks
1 medium onion, cut into thin wedges
½ teaspoon dry thyme
¼ teaspoon pepper
½ teaspoon salt
2 bay leaves
3 ½ cups water
2 packages chicken flavor Ramen noodles soup

In crock pot, layer sweet potatoes, onions and chicken. Sprinkle with thyme, pepper and salt. Add bay leaves. In a small bowl mix water (1 cup) and seasoning packet from Ramen noodles (reserve noodles). Pour over chicken and vegetables. Add remaining water, then cover. Cook on low 7 hours until vegetables and chicken are tender. Discard bay leaves. Stir in noodles. Cover and cook on high for 10 minutes. Stir well. Serve in bowl with hot crisp bread and a salad for a delicious and economical meal.

Frosty Gazpacho

2 medium ripe and firm tomatoes
1 large cucumber, peeled
1 rib celery
1 small vidalia onion

½ green bell pepper
½ red bell pepper
1 ½ cups tomato juice
1 tablespoon light olive oil
2 teaspoons fresh lemon juice
Avocado slices
Sour cream
Sage leaves or sprigs
1 teaspoon sugar or artificial sweetener
1 teaspoon Worcestershire sauce
½ teaspoon Tabasco sauce
2 teaspoons chopped Italian parsley
2 tablespoons red wine vinegar
1 small clove garlic, pressed
2 teaspoons chopped fresh cilantro
Salt to taste
¼ teaspoon ground pepper
½ teaspoon sugar
Chopped basil and cilantro
Lime wedges

Chop tomatoes, celery, cucumbers, onions and bell peppers into similar sized, chunky bits. Transfer mixture to a large bowl and combine with remaining ingredients. Refrigerate until cold. Transfer ⅓ of gazpacho mixture into a separate bowl and freeze mixture 45 minutes before serving time or until mixture starts to crystalize. Chill remaining Gazpacho until ready to serve. To serve, fill serving dishes with chilled Gazpacho and top with a scoop of the frozen Gazpacho and garnish around scoop with diced avocado, sour cream and lime slices. Sprinkle with basil and cilantro.

Serve 6

Ham and Lima Bean Soup

2 cups dried lima beans
8 cups cold water
1 ham bone (1 ½ - 2 pounds)
1 bay leaf
3 teaspoons salt
½ teaspoon sugar
1 cup sliced carrots
1 cup canned tomatoes
¼ cup chopped onion
¼ teaspoon fresh ground pepper
¼ teaspoon garlic powder

Wash beans and soak in water overnight. Add ham bone, bay leaf, salt and sugar. Cover and simmer 1 ½ hours or until beans are tender. Remove ham bone and 1 ½ cups of beans. Put remainder of beans and liquid in blender or processor for a coarse pulp. Combine whole beans, bean puree, carrots, onion and tomatoes. Cook until carrots are tender, about 15 minutes. Add pepper and garlic powder, stir and taste, adjust seasoning. Cut ham bits and add to soup. Serve with corn dodgers and green relish.

Mexican Chili

2 pounds ground chuck
¾ cup chopped green pepper
1 cup chopped onion
1 clove garlic, pressed
1 (16 ounce) can kidney beans, drained
2 (8 ounce) cans tomato sauce
1 (16 ounce) can tomatoes, not drained and chopped
1 fresh or canned green chiles, seeded and chopped
1 tablespoon plus 1 teaspoon of chili powder
2 teaspoons ground cumin
½ teaspoon dried whole basil
½ teaspoon salt

¼ teaspoon pepper
Pinch of sugar
¼ teaspoon hot sauce
Shredded cheddar cheese (optional)
Corn chips (optional)

Combine first four ingredients in a Dutch oven, cook over medium heat until meat is browned, stirring to crumble meat. Drain off drippings. Add kidney beans and next 10 ingredients. Cover, reducing heat and simmer 20 minutes, stirring occasionally. May be served with cheese and/or chips.

Taco Soup

1 pound ground chuck
1 large onion, chopped
3 (15 ½ ounce) cans Mexican-style chili beans, not drained
1 (15 ¼ ounce) can whole kernel corn, not drained
1 (15 ounce) can tomato sauce
1 (14 ½ ounce) can diced tomatoes, not drained
1 (4 ½ ounce) can chopped green chiles
1 (1 ¼ ounce) envelope taco seasoning mix
1 (1 ounce) envelope ranch style dressing mix
1 ½ cup water
Toppings: corn chips, shredded lettuce, chopped tomatoes, sour cream or cheese

Cook beef and onions in a Dutch oven over medium heat until meat is browned and onions tender, stirring until meat crumbles. Drain. Stir beans and next 7 ingredients into beef mixture. Bring to a boil. Reduce heat and simmer uncovered for 15 minutes, stirring occasionally. Spoon soup into bowls and top with desired toppings.

Turkey Vegetable Soup

1 turkey carcass cut in half
2 ½ quarts water
2 ribs celery, (with leaves) cut into 1-inch pieces
3 carrots, peeled and cut into 1-inch pieces
2 parsnips, peeled and cut into 1-inch pieces
1 cup tomatoes
2 medium onions, quartered
2 whole cloves garlic, pressed
6 whole peppercorns
1 teaspoon salt
¼ teaspoon sugar
4 sprigs fresh dill and two tablespoons chopped
¼ cup uncooked barley

Place carcass, water, celery, carrots, parsnips, tomatoes, onions, garlic, peppercorns, salt, sugar and dill sprigs in a large heavy soup pot. Bring to boil, reduce heat to a gentle simmer and cook for 30 minutes. Remove the carcass, celery leaves, and dill sprigs from the soup. Add the barley and simmer 40 minutes more, stirring occasionally, adding 2 tablespoons chopped dill during last 10 minutes. Taste and adjust seasonings.

Zucchini Soup

1 pound clean unpeeled zucchini
2 tablespoons green onions or leeks
1 clove garlic, minced
1 ¾ cups chicken broth
½ teaspoon salt
1 teaspoon curry powder
½ cup coffee cream

Chop unpeeled zucchini, green onions and garlic. Cook in heavy skillet for 10 to 15 minutes. Stir to keep from burning. Put all ingredients in blender and blend. Add cream. Serve hot with croutons or cold with minced chives.

This recipe is from Barbara Bush's book, "Reflections After the White House." She said that now everyone will know what to do with those extra zucchini, so freely given to you by friends.

Knife and Fork Sandwiches

(with one slice of bread)

No. 1 - Bacon and tomato with tossed salad

> 1 slice bread, toasted
> ¼ teaspoon mayonnaise and/or mustard
> 2 slices cooked bacon
> 1 slice tomato
> 1 slice cheese
> For garnish: shredded lettuce, green pepper, carrot and
>   onion

On ovenproof pie tin put toast, top with bacon, tomato and cheese; broil until cheese melts slightly. Transfer sandwich to plate and arrange salad ingredients around the open-faced sandwich. This makes a complete lunch and saves some calories, using one slice.

No. 2 - Ham and cheese with salad

> 1 thick slice of bread, toasted
> ¼ teaspoon honey mustard
> 1 slice precooked ham or slivered slices
> 1 slice of choice cheese
> For garnish: lettuce, chopped apple, raisins and nuts of
>   choice

On ovenproof pan place toast, ham and cheese; broil until cheese melts. Lift sandwich to plate and arrange salad ingredients around the sandwich.

No. 3 - Hamburger with mushrooms

½ toasted bun
1 hamburger patty, cooked as you like it
¼ cup sliced mushrooms
2 tablespoons Parmesan cheese
¼ teaspoon mayonnaise or mustard or both
Garnish: shredded lettuce, diced onion and tomato

On ovenproof pan place toasted bun half and spread with mayonnaise or mustard. Place hamburger patty on bun, top with mushrooms and the Parmesan cheese. Broil until the cheese melts. Lift to plate and garnish with salad as desired.

There are other choices: such as chicken breast; roast beef; corned beef; and kraut.

Curried B.L.T. Sandwiches

8 slices oatmeal bread, lightly toasted
Curry Spread
12 slices bacon, cooked and crumbled
¼ cup raisins
¼ cup cashew nuts, coarsely chopped
2 large tomatoes, sliced
Lettuce leaves

Coat one side of each slice with Curry Spread. Sprinkle bacon, raisins and nuts evenly on 4 slices; top each with tomato slices and a lettuce leaf. Cover with remaining 4 bread slices.

Curry Spread:

   2 tablespoons mayonnaise
   2 tablespoons sour cream
   1 tablespoon chutney
   1 teaspoon curry powder
   ¼ teaspoon grated orange rind
   Pinch of ginger
   Pinch of ground cumin

Kentucky Hot Brown

   8 slices white bread, sliced thick
   1 pound roasted turkey slices
   Cheese sauce (recipe follows)
   1 cup Parmesan cheese
   8 slices bacon, cooked
   2 large tomatoes, sliced and halved

Trim crust from bread slices and discard. Place bread on a baking sheet and broil 3 inches from heat until toasted, turning once. Arrange two slices in each of four lightly greased individual baking dishes. Top bread with turkey. Pour hot cheese sauce evenly over turkey and sprinkle with Parmesan cheese. Broil 6 inches from the heat for 4 minutes or until bubbly and lightly browned; remove from oven. Top evenly with bacon and tomato. Serve immediately.

Cheese Sauce:

   ½ cup butter or margarine
   ⅓ cup all-purpose flour
   3 ½ cups milk
   ½ cup shredded Parmesan cheese
   ½ teaspoon salt
   ¼ teaspoon fresh ground pepper
   Pinch of sugar

Melt butter in large sauce pan over medium heat. Whisk in flour and cook, whisking constantly, for 1 minute. Gradually whisk in milk. Bring to a boil and cook, whisking constantly, 1 to 2 minutes or until thickened. Whisk in cheese, salt, pepper and sugar. Remove from heat.

Quantity Version: Use a 15x10 inch pan and put the bread slices in bottom of pan. Top evenly with turkey slices and cheese sauce; sprinkle with the Parmesan cheese. Proceed as above.

Imogene's Pimento Cheese Spread

2 cups grated American cheese
2 teaspoons sugar
1 ¼ cups Miracle Whip Salad Dressing
½ jar of pimento

Mix well.

Imogene is known for her angel food cakes and then next is her pimento sandwiches that she has made by the dozens for many people.

Chapter Six - Main Dishes

The earth is full of the goodness of the Lord. Psalm 33:5

The main dish menus are varied. I hope some will suit you. I do admit that some are easier than others, but there is a time and place for all of them!

I'd like to point out that you will find some recipes that "USA Today" says are the healthiest because they contain the essential foods our genes crave for a long life. Thanks to Julie and Keith Stout for providing them. The two in this group are 15-Minute Chicken Chili and Grilled Salmon with Orange Glaze.

Included are a lot of chicken recipes. There are so many ways to prepare chicken, and I hope you will try some of them and find them a change from your on-hand recipes. Some are very simple and quick and easy to prepare. Others require a little longer time but are worth all the extra effort!

I think the time has come to serve seafood and fish more often! It is more plentiful in our stores than ever before. It is so healthy and it requires a short cooking time. I hope if you don't have a favorite recipe, you will try something from the fish and seafood recipes.

Special Bacon

6 thick slices bacon (I think peppered is best)
½ cup milk
½ cup flour, seasoned with salt and pepper
¼ cup oil for browning

Dip bacon slices in milk then flour. Place in a heavy skillet that has oil in it, over medium heat. Cook until brown and crispy. Drain on paper towel.

It is good with summer vegetables and makes a good bacon and tomato sandwich. It does not shrink! Try it soon!

Pork Loin Roast with Apricot/Orange Glaze

1 (4-5 lb.) loin roast
1 teaspoon salt
½ teaspoon pepper
2 cloves garlic
1 cup apricot marmalade
½ cup orange marmalade
1 can chicken broth

Salt and pepper the roast. Let set at room temperature 30 minutes. Place in a roaster bottom with rack or a large Pyrex with rack in bottom (a trivet type rack will work). Cook in preheated 500-degree oven for 10 minutes (this sears in the juices). Reduce heat to 350 degrees. Mix the garlic, marmalades and ¼ cup broth. Baste the roast often with this. Cook 35 minutes per pound. Remove and let rest at least 15 minutes before slicing. Use drippings scraped from bottom of cooker and rest of marmalade and ½ cup broth. If there is very much grease in pan, remove it first and then heat and serve as gravy for the roast. Taste and adjust seasoning.

I serve the sliced roast on a bed of spinach leaves and parsley and baked apricot halves and orange slices.

Serve 12

Ham and Turkey Roll-Ups

6 slices deli ham
6 slices deli roast turkey
3 slices Swiss cheese, room temperature
2 tablespoons horseradish mustard
2 tablespoons Hellmanns Mayonnaise
Green onion tops

102

After washing the green onion tops, wilt them in boiling water about 5 minutes. Drain on paper towel. Move them to cutting board and cut very thin ribbons.

Spread one side of turkey slices with mayonnaise and half the Swiss cheese slices. Put ½ slice in center of turkey slice; top with ham slice. Roll up lightly and put on plate. Repeat with other slices. After the rolls "have set" in refrigerator, take out and loosely tie onion tops around roll and curl the ends.

Make a sauce as follows to serve over the roll-ups:

> ½ cup mayonnaise
> ½ cup sour cream
> 2-3 tablespoons prepared horseradish
> ¼ cup milk
> 1 teaspoon sugar
> Salt and pepper to taste

Mix well and serve either heated or cold.

These are an easy "do-ahead" entrée for a buffet party. I usually alternate the ham and turkey slices, so some look like rolls of ham and some rolls of turkey. I also trim with scissors any rugged ends if necessary.

Crown Pork Roast

At first you may think this too difficult, but it really isn't and it makes a beautiful presentation (a similar one can be made from lamb). To make a nice presentation, you must order at least 12 chops from the rib end of a pork loin roast. This will be enough to make a nice crown. Salt and pepper well and stuff the crown with the following:

> Apple-raisin stuffing:
> 4 cups herb seasoned Pepperidge Farm stuffing
> ½ cup diced celery

1 apple diced
¼ cup raisins
¼ cup diced onion
1 egg beaten
½ cup chicken broth
Salt and pepper to taste

Mix all together, let set about 20 minutes, stir; if too dry add broth slowly. Stir and taste, adjust seasonings. Put into the crown of the roast.

Place the roast on a rack in uncovered roaster and place in a 325-degree oven allowing 35 minutes per pound, or until meat thermometer registers 170 degree internal temperature. Cut a piece of foil to cover the rib bones and the dressing, but leave the bottom part of the roast uncovered. Baste roast the last hour with drippings.

Transfer to platter and decorate platter with greens and spiced crabapples or apple wedges which have been glazed with sugar and butter.

Pan Gravy:

Drain off all fat except about 4 tablespoons from the roaster. Heat pan and scrape any bits. Add 4 cups liquid, part water and part broth. Mix 4 tablespoons cornstarch with ¼ cup cold water and add to the gravy. Add ½ teaspoon Kitchen Bouquet and salt and pepper to suit your taste.

Serve 12

Glazed Country Ribs

2 pounds country style pork ribs
1 ¾ teaspoon salt, divided
¼ teaspoon pepper
¾ cup orange juice
2 tablespoons lemon juice
½ cup firmly packed brown sugar

1 bay leaf
2 teaspoons garlic, pressed
1 teaspoons lemon zest
1 teaspoon ground ginger
¼ teaspoon ground cloves

Preheat oven to 400 degrees. Cut ribs into single rib portions and sprinkle both sides with salt and pepper (use half of amount indicated above).

Place ribs on a rack in a foil-lined shallow open roasting pan. Bake for 30 minutes. Reduce heat to 350 degrees. Turn ribs and bake 20 minutes longer. Pour off fat.

Meanwhile prepare sauce by combining in a medium saucepan the orange and lemon juices, brown sugar, bay leaf, garlic, lemon zest, spices and remaining salt and pepper. Bring to a boil.

Reduce heat and simmer, uncovered, until it is reduced to ½ cup, about 15 minutes. Brush glaze on pork ribs, return to oven for 10 minutes, turn and brush. Bake another 10 minutes until glazed.

Baked Ham with Cranberry Raisin Sauce

1 (5 pound) smoked fully cooked ham half
Whole cloves
1 (14 ounce) jar cranberry-orange sauce
½ cup raisins
1 teaspoon lemon juice
¼ teaspoon ground cinnamon

Slice skin from ham. Place ham, fat side up, on rack in a shallow roasting pan. Score fat in diamond design, and stud with cloves. Insert meat thermometer, making sure it does not touch bone or fat. Bake at 325 degrees for 1 ¾ hours. Remove ham from oven. Combine remaining ingredients; spread half of cranberry mixture over ham. Bake 20 minutes or until thermometer registers 140 degrees. Serve remaining sauce with ham.

Peachy Pork Chops

4 (1 inch thick) pork chops
¼ teaspoon seasoned salt
¼ teaspoon onion powder
1 (16 ounce) can sliced peaches, not drained
2 tablespoons brown sugar
¼ teaspoon dried basil
2 tablespoons butter or margarine

Place pork chops on a lightly greased rack or broiler pan. Sprinkle with seasoned salt and onion powder. Broil 4 inches from heat approximately 7 minutes on each side. Combine peaches and remaining ingredients in a small saucepan, stirring well. Cook, uncovered, over low heat 10 minutes, stirring often. Arrange chops on platter. Pour sauce over chops.

Hong Kong Pork Chops

2 loin or rib pork chops, 1 inch thick
1 teaspoon stir fry sauce or oyster sauce
1 tablespoon soy sauce
⅓ cup bread crumbs
⅛ teaspoon garlic powder
¼ teaspoon ground ginger
2 tablespoons dry onion soup mix

Combine sauces in a shallow bowl or pan. Combine crumbs, garlic powder, ginger and onion soup mix on waxed paper. Dip chops in sauce mixture, then in crumb mixture. Repeat again to double coat the chops. Place meaty side toward outside of dish on a cooking rack set in a 12x8 inch microwave-proof baking dish. Cover with paper towel. Microwave 16 to 18 minutes, rearranging chops once during cooking.

Broccoli Ham Roll-Ups

1 package (10 ounce) frozen chopped broccoli
1 can (10 ¾ ounce) condensed cream of mushroom soup, undiluted
1 cup dry breadcrumbs
¼ cup cheddar cheese
1 tablespoons onion, chopped
2 teaspoons pimento
⅛ teaspoon of each of the following: dried rosemary, thyme and essence, and fresh ground pepper
12 slices fully cooked ham, 1/8-inch thick

Cook broccoli according to package directions, drain. In a bowl combine soup, crumbs, cheese, onion, pimento and seasonings. Add broccoli and mix well. Spoon ¼ cup onto each ham slice, roll up and place in a non-greased 9x13x2 baking dish. Cover and bake at 350 degrees for 40 minutes or until heated through. These roll-ups can be frozen before baking. Take out as many as needed for a quick meal.

Ham Newburg in Patty Shells

2 tablespoons green pepper, chopped
2 tablespoons onion, chopped
2 tablespoons butter, melted
2 tablespoons flour
1 ½ cups half and half
¼ cup sherry cooking wine
3 egg yolks, beaten
2 cups cooked ham, diced
1 (4 ounce) can sliced mushrooms, drained
6 patty shells, cooked

Cook green peppers and onions in butter until tender. Stir in flour, stirring constantly; gradually add half and half. Cook stirring constantly until thickened. Stir in sherry. Stir a little hot mixture into the egg yolks and then stir the egg mixture back into the hot.

Cook, stirring until thickened. Stir in ham and mushrooms. Heat to serving temperature. To serve, pour into patty shells on plate and let some overflow. Sprinkle top with paprika and add a sprig of parsley.

When serving this for lunch or supper, I like to have a molded applesauce salad on lettuce leaf and asparagus spears on the plate with the Ham in Patty Shells.

Autumn Stuffed Pork Chops

¾ cup toasted raisin bread breadcrumbs
¼ cup diced unpeeled apple
¼ cup diced unpeeled pear
1 ½ tablespoons minced onion
1 tablespoon finely chopped celery
1 tablespoon butter or margarine, melted
½ teaspoon sugar
¼ teaspoon salt
Dash of pepper
Pinch of ground sage
4 (1 ¼ inch thick) pork chops, trimmed and cut with
   pockets
Salt and pepper
1 tablespoon butter or margarine, melted
2 tablespoons apple juice
1 tablespoon water
Glazed Apple Rings
Fresh sage leaves (optional)

Combine first 10 ingredients; stir well. Fill pockets of pork chops with stuffing mixture and secure with wooden picks. Sprinkle chops with salt and pepper. Brown chops on both sides in 1 tablespoon melted butter in a skillet. Add juice and water; cover, reduce heat and simmer 55 minutes or until chops are tender. Arrange the chops down the center of a serving platter; surround with Glazed Apple Rings. Garnish with fresh sage leaves, if desired.

Glazed Apple Rings

2 large red cooking apples (about 1 pound)
2 tablespoons lemon juice
¾ cup water
¼ cup sugar
2 tablespoons light corn syrup

Core apples. Slice apples into ½ inch thick rings; toss with lemon juice. Combine water, sugar, and syrup in a skillet; bring to a boil. Boil 2 minutes or until sugar dissolves, stirring constantly. Layer apple rings in skillet. Add any remaining lemon juice; reduce heat, and simmer 8 minutes or until rings are tender, turning once.

Honey Gingered Pork Tenderloin

2 (¾ pound) pork tenderloins
¼ cup honey
¼ cup soy sauce
¼ cup oyster sauce
2 tablespoons brown sugar
1 tablespoon plus 1 teaspoon minced fresh gingerroot
1 tablespoon minced garlic
1 tablespoon catsup
¼ teaspoon onion powder
¼ teaspoon ground red pepper
¼ teaspoon ground cinnamon
Fresh parsley sprigs (optional)

Place tenderloins in an 11x7x1 ½ inch baking dish. Combine honey and next 9 ingredients, stirring well; pour over tenderloins. Cover and marinate in refrigerator 8 hours, turning occasionally.

Remove tenderloins from marinade, reserving marinade. Grill tenderloins over medium-hot coals 25 to 35 minutes, turning often and basting with reserved marinade. Pork is done when meat thermometer inserted into thickest portion of tenderloin registers 160 degrees. To serve, slice tenderloins thinly and arrange on a serving platter. Garnish with fresh parsley, if desired.

Country Beef Wellington

1 pound ground beef
1 onion, minced
¼ cup green pepper, chopped
1 pound fresh mushrooms sliced
¼ cup Worcestershire sauce
2 cloves garlic, pressed
2 cups seasoned mashed potatoes (leftovers)
1 package puff pastry
2 tablespoons tomato paste
Shredded cheddar cheese

Cook beef and drain. Add onions and green pepper, cook 2 minutes and add garlic. In another skillet, add chopped mushrooms, onions, and Worcestershire sauce; cook until liquid evaporates. Add to meat and add 2 tablespoons tomato paste. Stir and taste for seasonings. Roll puff pastry and cut 6-inch rounds. Put egg wash all around edge. Put one serving of meat mushroom mixture on one half of the crust. Add 2 tablespoons mashed potatoes on top of meat mixture. Fold crust over and crimp with fork. When all are made, put on baking sheet and brush egg wash over all. Bake 25 minutes at 375 degrees. Take out and top with shredded cheddar cheese. Bake 5 minutes more. Serve with beef gravy, green salad, and garlic bread if desired.

This recipe came from Emeril on the food channel.

Beef and Vegetable Lasagna

2 tablespoons olive oil
1 pound ground round beef
4 cups tomato sauce
4 tablespoons chopped cilantro (or Italian parsley)
3 ½ cups low-fat ricotta cheese
1 cup chopped spinach, cooked and drained
¼ cup Parmesan cheese
1 tablespoon dried oregano
¾ teaspoon ground nutmeg
Freshly ground black pepper
8 lasagna noodles, cooked
3 cups grated low-fat mozzarella cheese

Preheat oven to 350 degrees. Heat oil in skillet over medium heat. Add ground beef and cook until browned. Drain. Place tomato sauce in a saucepan. Add browned beef and 2 tablespoons cilantro. Cook 5 minutes, remove from heat. In a bowl mix ricotta cheese, spinach, Parmesan cheese and remaining cilantro, oregano, nutmeg and pepper.

Place 2 cups tomato-meat sauce in bottom of a 9x13 dish. Place 4 lasagna noodles on top of sauce. Place half the ricotta mixture over all. Sprinkle with 1 cup mozzarella cheese. Repeat this one time. Top with remaining sauce and remaining cup mozzarella over top. Cover loosely with foil and bake 45 minutes. Remove foil and bake 20 minutes. Remove from oven and let rest 15 minutes before serving.

Taco Casserole

1 (10 ounce) package frozen mixed vegetables, thawed
2 pounds lean ground beef
½ cup onion, chopped
1 package taco seasoning
1 cup water

1 (10 ounce) can enchilada sauce (part salsa is okay)
2 cups shredded cheddar cheese
1 (10 ounce) bag of corn chips

Cook vegetables in microwave to barely thaw. Brown meat and onions, draining off fat. Add taco seasoning and water; cover and simmer 10 minutes. Remove from heat and stir in vegetables. Sprinkle corn chips on bottom of a 9x13 buttered casserole. Add half the meat mixture, top with half the sauce and sprinkle with half the cheddar cheese. Repeat each layer, beginning with corn chips and ending with cheese. Bake 15-20 minutes at 350 degrees. Serves 10 to 12.

This is my favorite ground beef casserole I believe, and it freezes well. I sometimes make it in smaller dishes and cook one and freeze one and feel so secure to have another dinner in the freezer!

Serves 10-12

Baked Steak

1 (4 pound) sirloin steak, 2 inches thick
1 large sweet onion, sliced
1 (4-6 ounce) can button mushrooms

For the sauce:

1 cup catsup
3 tablespoons Worcestershire sauce
3 tablespoons butter, melted
1 tablespoon lemon juice
½ teaspoon minced garlic (dry is alright)
1 (4 ounce) can of sliced mushrooms
Kitchen Bouquet as needed for brushing steak
Salt and pepper

Brush steak with Kitchen Bouquet and sprinkle with salt and pepper. Place on rack or broiler pan and place 3 inches from hot broiler unit, browning quickly on both sides. Remove from oven and pour off fat and remove from rack and place the steak in bottom of pan. Make the sauce and pour over steak. Arrange the onion slices and button mushrooms on top. Bake the steak at 350 degrees for about an hour.

Serves 6

Holiday Beef Tenderloin

1 tablespoon salt
1 ½ teaspoon onion powder
1 ½ teaspoon garlic powder
1 ½ teaspoon fresh ground pepper
1 teaspoon ground red pepper
½ teaspoon ground cumin
½ teaspoon nutmeg
1 (5 pound) beef tenderloin, trimmed well
¼ cup olive oil

Combine first seven ingredients. Rub tenderloin with oil and coat with spice mixture. Place in a roasting pan, cover and chill 8 hours. Bake at 500 degrees for 15 minutes, until browned. Lower temperature to 375 degree; bake 20 minutes or until desired degree or doneness. Let stand 10 minutes. Slice and serve with horseradish mayonnaise.

Serves 8

Roast Sirloin of Beef

(Most all the family members think this is the best meal possible)

1 (6 pound) beef rib roast
2 tablespoons olive oil
1 celery stalk, coarsely chopped
1 carrot, chopped
½ onion, chopped
1 bay leaf

3 fresh parsley sprigs
½ teaspoon thyme, crumbled
1 cup beef broth

Heat olive oil in heavy skillet over high heat. Season beef with salt and pepper and brown on all sides. Transfer beef to roasting pan and roast in preheated 450-degree oven for 20 minutes, basting occasionally with the pan juices. Reduce heat to 350 degrees and continue cooking until thermometer registers 120 degrees for rare, or about 1 hour. Meanwhile, take 3 tablespoons drippings from roaster to skillet and add all the seasoning ingredients listed above including the broth. Cook about 20 minutes. Transfer roast to cutting surface and let stand 20 minutes. Degrease the juices in pan; add stock mixture and bring to boil. Strain sauce. Transfer roast to warm platter and slice. Serve sauce separately.

8 Servings

Yorkshire Pudding

(Good served with Beef Roast)

1 cup sifted flour
1 cup milk
2 large eggs
½ teaspoon salt
3 teaspoons beef or bacon drippings

Combine first four ingredients in mixing bowl. Use electric mixer and beat mixture 5 minutes. Cover and refrigerate 1 hour. Preheat oven to 425 degrees. Put drippings into a 9x13 metal baking pan and heat until pan is very hot. Beat batter and pour into pan. Bake 20 minutes; lower oven to 375 degrees and continue baking until the pudding is puffed up and browned, about 15 minutes. Do not open door during cooking. Serve immediately.

Swiss Steak for Company

(John O. Flanary gave me this recipe)

6 pounds round steak, 2 inches thick
Salt and pepper
1 cup chopped onions
3 carrots cut into pieces
2 (6 ounce) cans tomato paste
2 (3 ounce) cans chopped mushrooms
1 (16 ounce) can sliced white potatoes, drained and diced
2 tablespoons Worcestershire sauce
2 teaspoons soy sauce
Red cooking wine

Pound salt and pepper and flour into meat. Brown on both sides, using fat trimmed from steak. Add chopped onions, brown slightly. Put meat and onions in a Dutch oven with carrots and cook slowly in 225-degree oven for 4-5 hours. When the meat is fork tender, take it out and add to pot the tomato paste, mushrooms, diced potatoes, the Worcestershire and soy sauce. Check and adjust seasoning. Cut the meat in serving pieces and add to the pot and cook another hour at 225 degrees. Add ¾ cup of red wine last few minutes to enhance the flavor. Serve with rice.

Deluxe Pot Roast

1 (4 to 5 pounds) boneless chuck roast
2 large cloves garlic, thinly sliced
½ teaspoon salt
Pinch of sugar
½ teaspoon pepper
¼ cup all-purpose flour
⅓ cup olive oil
1 medium onion, sliced
1 cup burgundy or other dry red wine
1 (8 ounce) can tomato sauce

1 tablespoon brown sugar
1 teaspoon dried whole oregano
1 teaspoon prepared horseradish
1 teaspoon prepared mustard
1 bay leaf
8 small red potatoes, peeled
6 carrots, scraped and quartered
4 stalks celery, cut into 2-inch pieces
Fresh oregano sprigs (optional)

Make lengthwise slits halfway through roast. Insert a garlic slice into each slit. Rub roast with salt and pepper; dredge in flour. Brown roast on all sides in hot oil in a large Dutch oven or skillet. Add sliced onion and wine to roast in Dutch oven.

Combine tomato sauce and next four ingredients; stir well. Pour over roast; add bay leaf. Bring liquid in Dutch oven to a boil; cover, reduce heat, and simmer 1 ½ hours. Add potatoes, carrots, and celery; cover and simmer 1 hour or until roast and vegetables are tender.

Transfer roast to a serving platter; spoon vegetables around roast, using a slotted spoon. Remove and discard bay leaf. Spoon any remaining pan drippings over roast and vegetables. Garnish roast with fresh oregano if desired.

Serves 8-10

No Peek Stew

2 pounds boneless stew meat
1 package Lipton's onion soup
1 can cream of mushroom soup
1 medium can mushrooms, pieces and stems
Pepper and salt
½ cup red wine or spicy tomato juice

Place in pot in order given, place tight fitting lid on pot and bake at 325 degrees for 3 hours. "Do not peek."

Thrifty Barbecued Beef

4 pounds beef shoulder or rump roast
3 cloves garlic, peeled and pressed
1 teaspoon salt
½ teaspoon pepper
1 teaspoon chili powder
1 teaspoon thyme
1 cup vegetable oil
½ cup red wine vinegar

In a bowl larger than the piece of meat, mix all other ingredients for a marinade. Pierce all over with cooking fork so seasoning will penetrate. Let stand in refrigerator several hours, turning often. Remove from marinade and pat dry. Barbecue 5-6 inches from hot coals for 30 minutes, turning to brown on all sides and brushing with marinade. Cover with dome top and continue turning and brushing for about 45 minutes. Remove meat from grill and let rest 10 minutes. Cut across grain in thin slices.

Beef and Mushroom Stew

½ cup all-purpose flour
1 ½ teaspoons salt
½ teaspoon black pepper
3 pounds lean boneless beef stew meat, cut into 1-inch
    cubes
4 tablespoons olive oil
1 large onion, coarsely chopped
2 cloves garlic, pressed
1 pound mushrooms, quartered
2 (13 ¾ ounce) cans reduced sodium beef broth
1 cup red burgundy wine
2 cups V8 juice
1 (1 pound) bag frozen pearl onions, thawed
1 (1 pound) bag peeled mini carrots, fresh or frozen,
    thawed

2 teaspoons dried thyme
1 teaspoon dried rosemary
2 bay leaves

Combine 4 tablespoons flour, 1 teaspoon salt and pepper in brown paper bag. Add half the beef at a time; shake until beef is lightly coated.

Heat 1 tablespoon oil in 5 quart Dutch oven over medium-high heat. Working in batches, brown beef, about 5 minutes, adding up to 2 tablespoons more oil as need. As they brown, transfer beef cubes to paper towel-lined platter.

Reduce heat to medium. Add chopped onion; sauté about 5 minutes or just until tender. Add garlic; sauté 2 minutes. Add mushrooms; sauté 5 minutes or just until mushrooms release their liquid. Using slotted spoon, transfer mushroom mixture to medium-size bowl. Cover and set aside.

Whisk together remaining flour, beef broth and burgundy wine and V8 juice in Dutch oven until smooth. Return beef to pan along with the pearl onions, carrots, thyme, rosemary and bay leaves. Bring to boiling, scraping up any browned bits from bottom of pan with wooden spoon. Reduce heat to low. Cover; simmer 45 minutes.

Uncover pot; simmer, stirring occasionally, for 55 minutes or until beef is tender. Stir in chopped onion-mushroom mixture 10 minutes before end of simmering. Remove stew from heat. Discard bay leaves. Stir in remaining ½ teaspoon salt.

Chicken in Sour Cream

3 pound chicken (cut up) or use 6 breast halves boned
2 tablespoons sherry cooking wine
1 tablespoon flour
½ teaspoon dry mustard
1 bouillon cube
2 tablespoons Parmesan cheese
1 teaspoon tomato paste

1 cup chicken stock
½ pint sour cream
Salt and fresh ground pepper

Brown chicken in butter. Pour hot wine over chicken. Remove chicken from pan. Add tomato paste, flour and seasonings. Stir until smooth, then add cream. Heat and return chicken to pan and simmer 30 to 40 minutes or until chicken is tender. Serve with rice.

This is a recipe from Lambuth Inn at Lake Junaluska, North Carolina. I ate it when I was attending the Jurisdiction School of Missions for United Methodist Women about 40 years ago, and I thought it so good that I asked for the recipe. I hope you will also enjoy it.

Easy Chicken in Microwave

4 boneless chicken breasts
½ stick margarine, melted
1 cup Italian dressing

Pound the chicken breasts to flatten and tenderize. Baste the chicken breasts in melted margarine. Pour Italian dressing over. Cover with plastic wrap and cook on high approximately 4-5 minutes.

My Oven Barbecued Chicken

2 (2 ½ -3 pound) fryers, cut up
½ cup catsup
⅓ cup vinegar
¼ cup brown sugar, packed
2 tablespoons margarine or butter
2 tablespoons Worcestershire sauce
2 tablespoons lemon juice
2 teaspoons salt

2 teaspoons chili powder
2 medium onions sliced, separated into rings
1-2 cloves of garlic, minced or pressed

Arrange chicken in a large baking pan and bake at 375 degrees for 40-45 minutes; drain. Put all other ingredients in saucepan. Bring to boil, reduce heat and simmer uncovered 10 minutes. Spoon over chicken and bake 10-15 minutes. Turn chicken, add more sauce and bake, continue to baste until chicken is tender.

Oven Barbecued Chicken

2 fryers (about 3 lbs each) quartered
2 cups bacon drippings
2 cups vinegar
½ cup white sugar
¼ cup brown sugar
2-3 pods dried hot pepper

Combine all ingredients except chicken; bring to boil. Lower heat and simmer while chicken browns. Season chicken with salt and flour and place skin side down in a well-greased roaster. Bake at 450 degrees until skin is as brown as you like. Turn chicken; baste generously with sauce. Reduce temperature to 350 degrees and continue basting often until all sauce is used. Bake until tender when tested with a fork through the thigh. If it browns too much, cover loosely with foil. Grease may be skimmed off of drippings, leaving a delicious sauce. The same sauce may be used for open-pit cooking, but do not flour the chicken.

Mrs. Ralph Porter won the outdoor cooking category with this recipe in the Evansville Courier in 1971. The recipe is from her Grannie Porter who had it handed down from her husband Ralph's family. Betty Porter said she tried using substitutes for the bacon drippings but she found that only the bacon drippings give the good flavor. I have used the recipe too and find it very good. For those who do not like tomatoes in barbecue sauce, they are sure to like it.

120

Oven Fried Chicken

6 drumsticks
4 chicken breast halves, with bone in
½ cup buttermilk
3 cups cornflake crumbs
2 teaspoons creole seasoning
¼ teaspoon freshly ground pepper
½ teaspoon garlic powder

In a large bowl add 1 quart water and 1 tablespoon salt and the chicken parts. Cover and refrigerate overnight or at least 8 hours. Drain chicken, rinse and pat dry. Place chicken in a shallow bowl; pour buttermilk over chicken, turning to coat.

Combine cornflakes, creole seasoning, pepper and garlic powder in plastic Ziploc bag. Put a few chicken pieces in bag and shake to coat. Remove chicken and repeat. Place chicken, bone side down in a jelly roll pan coated with cooking spray, and spray chicken with cooking spray. Use lowest rack in oven and bake 45 minutes at 400 degrees. Do not turn the chicken. 6-8 servings

Southern Fried Chicken

3 quarts water
1 tablespoon salt
1 (2 ½ pound) fryer chicken, cut up
1 teaspoon salt
1 teaspoon pepper
1 teaspoon paprika
Pinch of sugar
1 cup all-purpose flour
1 egg, beaten
½ cup milk
2 cups vegetable oil
½ cup bacon drippings

In a large bowl combine water, salt and cut up chicken. Cover and refrigerate at least 8 hours. Drain chicken, rinse with cold water and pat dry. Combine 1 teaspoon salt, pepper, paprika, sugar, and flour in a large plastic Ziploc bag. Dip chicken pieces in the beaten egg and milk, then put a few pieces at a time in the bag and shake. Combine the oil and bacon drippings in a large cast iron skillet, heat to 360 degrees. Put chicken pieces in gently, and cover. Cook 6 - 8 minutes more. Remove lid and cook about 8 minutes, turning as it browns. Drain on paper sack (if available). Serve with chicken gravy and hot biscuits. 4-5 servings

Fried Chicken Gravy

¼ to ½ cup drippings and scrapings from fried chicken
   skillet
¼ cup flour
2 cups warm milk
¼ teaspoon salt
¼ teaspoon pepper

Put the drippings in the skillet over medium heat; add flour, stirring until brown. Gradually add the warm milk and continue to cook and stir until thickened and bubbly. Add salt and pepper and taste and adjust if needed.

Baked Chicken Breast with Ham

8 chicken breasts halves, skinned and boned
8 small slices country ham
8 slices Swiss cheese
1 (10 ¾ ounce) can cream of chicken soup, undiluted
½ cup cooking white wine
1 cup herb seasoned breadcrumbs
Melted butter

Arrange chicken breasts in a 9x13 baking dish, lightly sprayed. Top with ham slices, then top with cheese. Combine soup and wine. Spoon liquid over the chicken. Sprinkle with the breadcrumbs and drizzle with melted butter. Cover with foil and bake in preheated 350 degree oven 45 to 50 minutes. Sprinkle with paprika. Take foil off the last 10 minutes of cooking and spoon sauce over chicken. 8 servings

Stuffed Chicken Breasts

2 large chicken breast halves, skinned and boned
¼ cup chopped onion
3 tablespoons chopped green pepper
1 clove garlic, pressed or minced
2 tablespoons butter or margarine, melted
⅔cup herb-seasoned stuffing mix
⅓ cup water
¼ teaspoon salt
¼ teaspoon fresh ground pepper
2 tablespoons butter or margarine, melted
½ cup cream of chicken soup, undiluted
2 tablespoons white cooking wine
1 tablespoon stuffing mix

Place each piece chicken between 2 sheets wax paper; flatten to ¼ inch, using mallet or rolling pin. Set aside. Sauté onion, green pepper, and garlic in 2 tablespoons butter. Stir in ⅔ cup stuffing mix and next three ingredients. Spread stuffing mix evenly on each chicken breast, leaving a ½ inch margin all around. Fold short ends of chicken over stuffing; roll up, beginning with one unfolded side. Secure with wooden picks.

Brown chicken in 2 tablespoons butter in a 9-inch pie plate. Combine soup and wine; pour over chicken. Sprinkle with rest of stuffing. Cover with foil and bake at 325 degrees for 50 minutes or until done. Garnish with parsley.

Chicken Divan Casserole

2 (10 ounce) packages frozen broccoli
4 cooked chicken breasts, boned and sliced
2 cups condensed cream of chicken soup
1 cup mayonnaise
1 teaspoon lemon juice
½ teaspoon curry powder
½ cup sharp cheddar cheese, shredded
½ cup chopped almonds, toasted

Cook broccoli until crisp tender, drain and arrange in bottom of 11x4x2 casserole. Place chicken on top of broccoli. Combine soup, mayonnaise, lemon juice and curry powder and pour over the chicken. Sprinkle with cheese, top with almonds and bake at 350 degrees for 20 to 25 minutes. Decorate with pimento strips and sprigs of cilantro. Serve 6 to 8

Extra Special Chicken Casserole

½ pound fresh mushrooms, sliced
3 tablespoons butter
3 whole chicken breasts, boned and sliced
1 teaspoon salt
½ teaspoon fresh ground pepper
½ cup oil
1 ½ cups rice, uncooked
1 garlic clove, pressed
3 cups chicken broth
1 jar white onions
½ cup cooking sherry
½ cup slivered almonds

Sauté mushrooms in butter. Remove from pan. Season chicken with salt and pepper and brown in half the oil. Remove chicken and brown rice and garlic in remaining oil. Stir in 2 cups chicken broth. Turn into a 9 x 13 casserole. Arrange chicken, onion, and mushrooms on rice. Mix remaining broth with the cooking wine and pour over chicken. Cover and bake at 350 degrees for 45 minutes. Uncover and bake 25 minutes. Sprinkle almonds over top. Serve 6

Shrimp and Chicken Casserole

1 (2 ½-3 pound) broiler-fryer (or 4 cups chopped cooked chicken)
½ teaspoon salt
½ teaspoon garlic salt
1 pound unpeeled medium sized fresh shrimp
2 (16 ounce) packages frozen broccoli cuts, thawed and drained
1 cup mayonnaise
1 (10 ¾ ounce) can cream of chicken soup, undiluted
1 (10 ¾ ounce) can cream of celery soup, undiluted
3 tablespoons lemon juice
½ teaspoon fresh ground pepper
1 cup shredded cheddar cheese
½ cup herb seasoned crumbs
1 tablespoon butter, melted
Garnish with paprika, shrimp and parsley sprigs

Combine chicken and salts in pan or Dutch oven; add water to cover and bring to a boil. Cook until tender, about 45 minutes. Bone chicken, cut in bite size pieces, and set aside. Bring 4 cups of water to boil and add shrimp and cook 3-5 minutes until pink. Drain well, rinse in cold water. Peel and de-vein shrimp. Save three for garnish.

Spread broccoli in sprayed 13x9x2 baking dish, set aside. Combine mayonnaise and next four ingredients; spread over broccoli. Set aside remaining sauce. Combine chicken and shrimp; spread evenly over casserole and top with remaining sauce. Cover and chill 8 hours. Remove from refrigerator and let stand at room temperature 30 minutes. Cover and bake at 350 degrees for 30 minutes. Uncover, sprinkle with cheese. Combine crumbs and butter, sprinkle over cheese and cook 15 minutes until hot and bubbly. Sprinkle paprika, add any garnish.

Rotel Chicken

Several years ago, Karen Stone was chairperson of membership nurture and outreach in the local United Methodist Women, and she promoted a luncheon for the ladies and served this dish. I think it is one of the very best chicken casserole dishes, and with her permission I'm sharing it.

4 whole chicken breasts
1 (12 ounce) package vermicelli
2 green peppers, chopped
2 medium onions, chopped
1 ½ sticks margerine
1 can Rotel tomatoes (whole)
1 large can Leseur peas (I sometimes use frozen)
2 pounds velveeta cheese, diced
1 large can sliced mushrooms
2 tablespoons Worcestershire sauce

Cook chicken and chop. Chop and sauté onions in margarine. Add peppers, Rotel tomatoes, and Worcestershire sauce. Add diced cheese, peas and mushrooms. Drain both and save liquid as it may be needed to make a better consistency. Cook pasta in the chicken broth, drain, and add chicken. Salt and pepper to taste. Put in casserole and bake 30 minutes at 350 degrees. It will make a generous 13x9 casserole or two 9x9 casseroles.

Creamy Chicken Tetrazzini

4 cups chicken breast, chopped or shredded
1 teaspoon salt
1 teaspoon pepper

1 (8 ounce) package spaghetti
1 large green pepper, chopped
1 cup sliced fresh mushrooms
1 small onion, chopped
¼ cup butter or margarine, melted
¼ cup all-purpose flour
½ teaspoon salt
½ teaspoon garlic powder
½ teaspoon poultry seasoning
½ teaspoon pepper
1 cup half-and-half
2 (8 ounce) cups shredded sharp cheddar cheese, divided
1 (10 ¾ ounce) can cream of mushroom soup, undiluted
¾ cup grated Parmesan cheese, divided
¼ cup sherry
1 (4 ounce) jar sliced pimento, drained
1 teaspoon paprika
¾ cup sliced almonds, toasted

Place chicken in a Dutch oven and cover with water. Add 1 teaspoon salt and 1 teaspoon pepper, and bring to a boil. Cover, reduce heat, and simmer 1 hour or until chicken is tender. Remove chicken from broth, reserving broth. Let chicken cool to touch. Bone and coarsely shred chicken.

Add enough water to reserved broth to measure 3 quarts. Bring to a boil. Cook spaghetti in broth according to package directions. Drain and set aside.

Sauté green pepper, mushrooms and onion in butter in a Dutch oven until tender. Add flour and next four ingredients; stir until smooth. Cook 1 minute, stirring constantly. Gradually stir in half-and-half, and cook until thickened, stirring gently. Add ¾ cup cheddar cheese, stirring until cheese melts. Add shredded chicken, mushroom soup, ½ cup Parmesan cheese, sherry and pimiento; stir well.

Combine chicken mixture with cooked spaghetti, tossing gently until thoroughly combined. Spread mixture in a greased

13x9x2 inch-baking dish. Bake uncovered at 350 degrees for 20 to 25 minutes, or until thoroughly heated. Combine remaining ¼ cup Parmesan cheese and 1 teaspoon paprika; stir well. Sprinkle remaining 1 ¼ cups cheddar cheese in diagonal rows across top of casserole. Repeat procedure with sliced almonds and Parmesan-paprika mixture. Bake an additional 5 minutes or until cheddar cheese melts. 6-8 servings

Chicken Noodle Casserole

4 cups diced cooked chicken
½ cup diced onion
1 cup celery, diced
3-4 cups frozen mixed vegetables, barely cooked
2 ½ cups milk
1 cup Parmesan cheese
2 (8 ounces) Philadelphia cream cheese, diced
Tabasco, salt and pepper
1 package narrow noodles cooked per instructions

Whip together cheeses, pepper and milk. Mix all ingredients together and put in buttered casserole. Bake at 350 degrees for approximately 45 minutes to an hour. Before finished, sprinkle top with Parmesan, almonds and dribble butter.

Chicken and Artichokes

4 boned chicken breast halves
9 tablespoons butter or margarine (divided)
1 cup fresh mushrooms
½ onion, diced
1 garlic clove, pressed
¼ cup white cooking wine
¼ cup flour
1 ½ cups milk (or cream will make it better)

2 (14 ounce) cans artichoke hearts, drained and chopped
¼ cup Parmesan cheese
½ teaspoon salt
Fresh ground pepper
1 teaspoon chopped fresh parsley

Cut chicken breast into strips and set aside. Melt 3 tablespoons butter in skillet over medium heat; add mushrooms, onion, and sauté 6 minutes. Add garlic and cook 2 minutes. Remove this mixture from skillet.

Melt 2 tablespoons butter in same skillet, add chicken strips and cook 10 minutes or until tender. Stir in wine and cook 5 minutes. Return mushroom mixture to skillet, stirring well. Remove from heat.

Melt 4 tablespoons butter in a small saucepan. Whisk in flour until smooth. Gradually add milk and cook, whisking for 5 minutes or until it thickens. Stir in artichokes and next three ingredients. Spoon chicken mixture into 11x7 dish and top with the artichoke mixture. Bake at 300 degrees for 20 minutes till bubbly. Sprinkle parsley on top.

Serve 4

The Linda Walsh

4-5 pounds breast of chicken, skinned and boned
1 can cream of chicken soup
1 can cream of mushroom soup
1 (3 ounce) container of sour cream
1 package ready-mix chicken stuffing

Simmer chicken in water to cover until cooked. Reserve liquid, cool and remove fat. Lay bite-size pieces of chicken in a flat baking dish or casserole. Mix the soups and sour cream, spread over the chicken.

Make the stove top stuffing as directed, but use two cups of the reserved liquid instead of water. Flavor the dressing generously with poultry seasoning and thyme. Spread over chicken and bake 35-40 minutes in a 325-degree oven.

This recipe is from Barbara Bush's book "Reflections after the White House." Linda Walsh is a friend and summer resident at Kennebunkport and thus the name that Barbara Bush gave to the dish.

Mexican Chicken Bake

4 boneless, skinless chicken breasts
½ cup Hellmann's mayonnaise
¾ cup seasoned breadcrumbs
1 cup chunky salsa
1 cup shredded Monterey Jack cheese

Preheat oven to 425 degrees. Brush chicken on all sides with mayonnaise then dip into breadcrumbs.

Arrange chicken in a 13x9 baking dish. Bake 15 minutes. Top with salsa then cheese. Bake 5 more minutes or until cheese is melted and chicken is done. Serve with Mexican rice.

Upper-Crust Chicken

10 slices white bread (day old)
2 cups cooked chicken, chopped
1 cup celery slices
2 cups sharp cheddar cheese, shredded
1 cup mayonnaise
2 eggs, slightly beaten
½ teaspoon salt
½ teaspoon poultry seasoning
1 ½ cups milk

Trim and reserve crusts from bread. Cut bread slices diagonally into quarters. Cut crust into cubes. Combine cubes, chicken, celery and 1 ¾ cup cheese and 1 cup milk. Mix well and spoon into 11x7 baking dish. Arrange bread quarters over chicken mixture. Combine mayonnaise, eggs, and seasonings. Mix well. Gradually add rest of milk, mixing until blended. Pour over bread and sprinkle with remaining cheese. Cover and refrigerate several hours or overnight. Bake uncovered at 375 degrees for 30 minutes.   8 servings

I use this easy casserole with leftover turkey or chicken. It has a nice crusty top.

"Don't Peek" Baked Chicken and Rice

1 (2 ½ - 3 pound) chicken, cut up
1 can of celery soup
1 can of mushroom soup
1 cup water, cold
1 cup long, uncooked rice
1 package dry onion soup mixture

Mix rice in between respective layers of soups; add water to each and season to taste. Sprinkle with the dry onion soup mixture. Lay cut-up pieces of chicken on top. Cover the whole casserole very tightly with foil and place in an oven at 250 degrees. Bake for two hours and do not peek until two hours are up. Delicious!

15-Minute Chicken Chili

1 tablespoon canola oil, or extra virgin olive oil
10 ounces boneless, skinless chicken breast, cut into bite-size pieces
1 ½ tablespoons chili powder
1 ½ tablespoons cumin
2 (14 ½ ounce) can no-salt added diced tomatoes

1 (15 ounce) can no-salt added black or red beans
1 (4 ½ ounce) can minced green chiles
1 cup yellow whole-kernel corn, frozen or canned
Salt and cayenne pepper to taste

In a medium saucepan, sauté chicken in oil over medium heat for 3 minutes or until white. Stir in chili powder and cumin to coat chicken. Sauté 3-4 minutes. Add remaining ingredients and heat through.   Serves 4

This is a recipe recommended by "USA Weekend" as one of the six healthiest recipes, for it contains some of the foods that our genes crave for a long life.

Chicken Stir-Fry

⅓ cup fresh orange juice
¼ cup soy sauce
1 teaspoon cornstarch
¼ teaspoon grated orange peel
Fresh ground pepper
1 pound boneless, skinless chicken breast, sliced
¼ cup water
3 cups small broccoli pieces
2 teaspoons vegetable oil
1 teaspoon fresh ginger or ½ teaspoon powdered

Combine first five ingredients in bowl. Stir in chicken and let stand 10 minutes. Bring water to a boil in non-stick skillet. Add broccoli, cover and steam 3 minutes. Drain and reserve. Heat oil in same skillet and add chicken and marinade and ginger, stirring for 4 to 5 minutes. Stir in broccoli. Serve with chow-mein noodles.

Chicken and Broccoli Alfredo

6 ounces uncooked fettuccine
1 cup fresh or frozen broccoli flowerettes
2 tablespoons butter or margarine
1 pound skinless, boneless chicken breast, cubed
1 (10 ¾ ounce) can mushroom soup
½ cup Parmesan cheese
½ cup milk
¼ teaspoon fresh ground pepper
Pinch sugar

Prepare fettuccine according to package directions. Add broccoli for last 4 minutes of cooking time. Drain. In skillet over medium heat, heat butter. Add chicken and cook until browned, stirring often. Add soup, milk and cheese, pepper, sugar, and fettuccine mixture and cook, stirring often until heated well.

Roast Turkey
With Wild Rice and Pecan Stuffing

1 (14-16 pound) turkey
3 tablespoons butter
1 tablespoon honey
½ teaspoon fresh ground pepper
½ teaspoon salt
2 cups broth
½ cup water

Stuffing:

7 cups chicken stock or broth
1 ½ cups wild rice
1 ½ cups long grain white rice
½ cup melted butter
2 medium onions, chopped
1 ½ cups celery, chopped

1 can sliced mushrooms
2 large garlic cloves, minced
1 teaspoon poultry seasoning
¼ cup cooking white wine
2 eggs, beaten
1 cup chopped pecans
¼ cup chopped parsley
½ teaspoon pepper

Gravy:

4 cups broth and stock
¼ cup butter
6 tablespoons flour
Salt and pepper to taste

For turkey:

Preheat oven to 425 degrees. Spoon stuffing into neck and cavities. Skewer openings and place turkey on rack in large roasting pan. Melt butter in small saucepan, add honey, salt and pepper. Brush mixture over turkey. Pour stock and water into pan. Roast 45 minutes. Reduce heat to 350 degrees. Cover turkey with foil and continue cooking until thermometer registers 175 degrees (about 2 hours and 20 minutes), add more water if needed.

For stuffing:

Bring stock to boil and add wild rice. Reduce heat, cover and simmer 30 minutes. Add long-grain rice. Cover and cook until rice is tender, and stock is absorbed, about 20 minutes. Transfer to large mixing bowl.

Melt ½ cup butter in large skillet over medium heat. Add onions and celery and sauté 10 minutes. Add mushrooms, seasoning, and garlic, cooking until tender (about 8-10 minutes). Add wine, bringing to a boil. Pour this mixture over rice. Stir in eggs, remaining stock, pecans and parsley. Adjust salt and pepper to taste.

For gravy:

Pour pan juices into measuring cup. Degrease juices. Add enough stock to make 4 ½ cups. Melt butter in large saucepan over low heat. Add flour and stir until golden brown, approximately 5 minutes. Gradually whisk in stock and bring to a boil. Reduce heat and simmer until thickened. Season to taste with salt and pepper.

My Cornbread Dressing

6 cups cornbread crumbs
2 cups homemade breadcrumbs
2 cups chicken broth and/or turkey broth
1 teaspoon salt
½ teaspoon fresh ground pepper
1 ½ teaspoon poultry seasoning
2 medium onions chopped
4 stalks celery
¼ cup butter or margarine
3 eggs lightly beaten

I toast the crumbs in a large deep baking pan in the oven with the broil unit on. Stir frequently and when they are toasted and dried a bit, I put the crumbs in a large crockery mixing bowl. Sauté the onion and celery in butter. Add to the crumbs and all the other ingredients. Taste for seasoning. Spoon the dressing in pone like shapes into a sprayed 9x13 Pyrex baking dish. Bake at 375 degrees for about 25 minutes.

Trout Almondine

2 pounds trout fillets
Salt and fresh ground pepper
1 egg
1 cup milk
Flour

½ cup butter
⅓ cup slivered almonds
1 tablespoon lemon juice
2 tablespoons Worcestershire sauce
1 tablespoon chopped parsley

Salt and pepper the fillets. Beat together egg and milk. Dip trout in egg mixture. Drain and dredge in flour. Melt butter in skillet. Sauté trout about 6-8 minutes, until golden brown. Remove trout to warm platter. Add almonds to skillet and brown lightly, add lemon juice and Worcestershire sauce, heat through. Pour over fish.

I would serve a sliced baked potato, steamed broccoli and a tossed salad with raspberry vinaigrette dressing. Lemon dessert is always good after a fish dinner as well.

Serves 4

Grilled Salmon with Orange Glaze

¼ cup orange marmalade
2 teaspoons sesame oil
2 teaspoons reduced-sodium soy sauce
½ teaspoon grated fresh ginger root
1 garlic clove, pressed or crushed
3 tablespoons rice vinegar
1 pound boneless, skinless salmon fillets cut into 4 pieces
6 scallions, thinly sliced (substitute green onions, thinly sliced)
¼ teaspoon sesame seeds, toasted (optional)

Combine marmalade, oil, soy sauce, ginger, garlic and vinegar. Heat grill. Brush glaze on each side of salmon; grill about 5 minutes on each side. Top with scallions and sesame seeds. Serves four

This is the recipe from "USA Weekend" that is one of the six healthiest recipes.

Planked Salmon
A Meal Served on a Plank

6 salmon steaks
6 medium size tomatoes (firm)
1 package chopped frozen spinach, microwaved and seasoned
1 (10 ounce) package frozen peas
6 small yellow onions
6 cups riced and seasoned potatoes
3 cups sauce (recipe follows)

To poach salmon use 4 cups water, 1 lemon sliced, 1 carrot sliced, 1 stalk celery sliced and 1 teaspoon peppercorns. Bring to boil and simmer 10 minutes, add salmon steaks and simmer another 10 minutes. Remove skillet from heat and let stand 8 minutes. Move salmon to platter and keep warm.

Cut tops from tomatoes, spoon out some of pulp. Invert to drain juice, and then cook in microwave 4-5 minutes. Then stuff tomatoes with the cooked spinach. Partially cook the onions and peas separately in microwave and season lightly with salt, pepper and melted butter.

At dinnertime, place potatoes in pastry bag with large tip and pipe around boards (I use individual boards rather than one large board. The guests eat from the board placed on an ovenware plate). Put other items on plank and pour some sauce on steak, onions and the bare spots on board. Top with Parmesan cheese. (Do not put sauce on tomatoes or peas.)

Marguery Sauce:

1 tablespoon chopped parsley
3 green onions, chopped
1 clove garlic, pressed
1 rib celery, chopped
2 tablespoons butter
1 can shrimp
½ cup chopped mushrooms
3 tablespoons butter

3 tablespoons flour
1 ½ cups milk
¼ cup sauterne wine
¼ teaspoon nutmeg
Salt and pepper to taste

Sauté parsley, onions, garlic, and celery in butter; simmer until tender. Add shrimp and mushrooms. Make a cream sauce with other ingredients and combine all together.

Put sauce on plank over salmon and onions. Sprinkle with Parmesan cheese and place plank in preheated oven about 5 inches from boiler. This will take 5 to 10 minutes. You may need to put pieces of foil on spinach to keep from burning. The potatoes need to brown lightly and the sauce bubble.

This makes a lovely presentation at a sit down dinner. It sounds like a lot of trouble but it is worth it. The planks are available at restaurant supply stores. The foods can be prepared ahead and even put on boards ahead. I keep the sauce to put on last. I serve a fruit salad and that is all that's really needed. Sometimes I serve French bread (baked in flower pots when I want to be real fancy). Steaks, meatloaf, and other types of firm seafood may be used.

Salmon Mouse

¼ cup cold water
1 envelope plain gelatin
¼ cup chili sauce
1 cup sour cream
1 (8 ounce) Neufchatel cream cheese, softened
1 teaspoon mixed herbs
¼ teaspoon black pepper
1 can salmon, skinless, boneless and flaked
1 hard boiled egg, peeled and diced
¼ cup chopped celery
¼ cup pimento-stuffed green olives, chopped

138

Spray fish mold or other decorative mold. Put cold water in saucepan; sprinkle gelatin on top. Let stand 1 minute to soften. Add chili sauce. Cook over medium heat 5 minutes until gelatin is completely dissolved. Transfer to mixing bowl, add cheese, herbs and pepper. Mix on high until creamy, fold in salmon, egg, celery and olives. Spoon into mold. Cover with plastic and refrigerate at least 3 hours. Remove from mold. Put one slice of stuffed olive for eye if using a fish mold and decorate with parsley, chives (if available) and lemon slices.

Scalloped Oysters

4 (12 ounce) containers fresh oysters
½ pound butter crackers, crumbled
½ pound plain soda crackers, crumbled
1 stick butter
About 1 to 1 ½ cups heavy cream
½ teaspoon fresh ground pepper

Drain oysters, reserving liquid, mix cracker crumbs. Place ⅓ of the crumbs in bottom of a shallow buttered casserole. Add a layer of half the oysters, sprinkle with pepper and dot with ½ of butter. Make another layer and top with crumbs, dot with rest of butter. Combine oyster liquid and cream and pour over casserole, taking a spoon to make a hole so liquid can pour down through. Bake at 400 degrees 25-30 minutes.

This is a must for the Thanksgiving and Christmas dinners.

Baked Flounder

4 flounder fillets (about ¼ pound each)
2 tablespoons chopped onion
½ teaspoon salt
¼ teaspoon freshly ground pepper

139

⅓ cup apple juice
2 tablespoons cooking sherry wine
2 tablespoons lemon juice
2 tablespoons butter
2 tablespoons flour
¼ cup whipping cream
¼ cup fresh grated Parmesan cheese
Fresh parsley

Arrange fillets in lightly sprayed 12x8x2 baking dish. Sprinkle with onion, salt and pepper. Combine apple juice, wine and lemon juice; pour over fish. Cover and bake 25 minutes or until fish flakes easily when forked. Transfer to serving platter. Strain and reserve ⅔ cup liquid. Melt butter in heavy saucepan over low heat; add flour, stirring until smooth. Cook 1 minute, stirring constantly. Gradually add whipping cream and the ⅔cup liquid. Cook, stirring constantly until sauce thickens and bubbles. Pour over fish. Sprinkle with cheese and parsley.

Microwave directions:
Arrange fillets, thicker portions to outside. Sprinkle with the chopped onions, salt and pepper. Combine juice, wine and lemon juice and pour over fish. Cover with heavy duty plastic wrap, fold back corner for steam to escape. Microwave on high 8 to 10 minutes or until fish flakes easily. Transfer to serving platter. Strain ⅔ cup of liquid. Place butter in a 2 cup glass measure and microwave on high 45 seconds until melted. Add flour, stir until smooth. Gradually add whipping cream and reserved liquid, stir well. Microwave on high 3 minutes or until thickened and bubbly, stirring at 1-minute intervals. Pour over fish. Sprinkle with Parmesan cheese and parsley.

Poached Salmon / Horseradish Sauce

4 cups water
1 lemon, sliced
1 carrot, sliced
1 stick celery, sliced

1 teaspoon peppercorns
4 (4 ounce) salmon steaks

Combine first five ingredients in a large skillet; bring to a boil over high heat. Cover, reduce heat and simmer 10 minutes. Add salmon steaks and simmer 10 minutes. Remove from heat and let stand 8 minutes. Remove salmon steaks to serving plate. Serve with horseradish sauce.

Horseradish Sauce:

¼ cup mayonnaise
¼ cup plain yogurt
2 teaspoons prepared horseradish
1 ½ teaspoons lemon juice
1 ½ teaspoons chopped chives or green onions

Combine all ingredients; cover and chill.

Seafood Mornay

1 ¼ pounds large fresh shrimp, peeled and deveined
½ pound fresh sea scallops
½ cup Chablis or other dry white wine
12 ounces crab meat
½ cup dry vermouth
¼ cup plus 2 tablespoons butter or margarine
1 tablespoon finely chopped onion
¼ cup all-purpose flour
2 cups milk
⅔ cup grated Parmesan cheese
½ cup (2 ounces) shredded Gruyere cheese
½ cup (2 ounces) shredded Swiss cheese
¼ teaspoon salt
¼ teaspoon pepper
⅛ teaspoon ground nutmeg
½ cup herbed breadcrumbs

141

¼ cup butter or margarine, melted
⅛ teaspoon paprika
2 tablespoons chopped fresh parsley

Poach shrimp and scallops in white wine 3 to 4 minutes; drain well. Repeat procedure with oysters and vermouth. Combine seafood, and spoon mixture into four individual baking dishes. Melt ¼ cup plus 2 tablespoons butter in a heavy saucepan; add onion, and sauté until tender. Add flour, stirring until smooth. Cook 1 minute, stirring constantly. Gradually add milk; cook over medium heat, stirring constantly, until thickened and bubbly. Add cheeses, stirring until melted. Stir in salt, pepper, and nutmeg. Spoon sauce evenly over seafood. Combine breadcrumbs and ¼ cup melted butter; stir well, and sprinkle over sauce. Sprinkle with paprika. Bake, uncovered, at 350 degrees for 20 to 25 minutes. Garnish with parsley. Yield: 4 servings.

Salmon Croquettes

¼ cup finely chopped onion
¼ cup butter or margarine, melted
⅛ cup all-purpose flour
⅛ cup meal
1 cup milk
½ teaspoon salt
⅛ teaspoon pepper
½ teaspoon dry dill weed
⅛ teaspoon ground red pepper
⅛ paprika
1 (15 ½ ounce) can pink salmon
1 ½ cups fine, dry breadcrumbs, divided
2 ½ teaspoons lemon juice
1 egg, beaten
Vegetable oil
Cucumber Sauce
Fresh dillweed sprigs (optional)

Sauté onion in butter in a saucepan over low heat until tender. Add flour; stir until smooth. Cook 1 minute, stirring constantly. Gradually add milk; cook over medium heat, stirring constantly, until thickened and bubbly. Stir in salt and next four ingredients. Remove from heat; set aside.

Drain salmon; remove and discard skin and bones. Flake salmon with a fork. Combine salmon, reserved sauce, ½ cup breadcrumbs, and lemon juice; stir well. Cover and chill. Shape mixture (with floured hands) into 12 croquettes. Roll each croquette in remaining 1 cup breadcrumbs; dip in egg, and roll again in breadcrumbs. Fry in deep hot oil (375 degrees) until golden. Drain on paper towels. Serve immediately with Cucumber Sauce. Garnish with dillweed, if desired.   Yield: 4 servings.

Note: they may be baked in oven at 375 degrees for 20 to 30 minutes.

Cucumber Sauce:

    ½ cup unpeeled, seeded and chopped cucumber
    ½ cup mayonnaise
    ½ cup sour cream
    1 tablespoon minced fresh chives
    1 teaspoon minced fresh parsley
    ¼ to ½ teaspoon minced fresh dillweed
    ¼ teaspoon salt
    4 lemon baskets

Chapter Seven – Bread, Rolls, Muffins, & Waffles

"I am the bread of life. He who comes to me will never go hungry, and he who believes in me will never be thirsty." John 6:35

Nothing says "Welcome" quite like the aroma of fresh baked bread. I've included the bread recipes that I bake the most often. Bread making and sharing is one of my great pleasures.

Flower Pot Bread

To season flower pots for baking:

The pots I have are about three inches high and three inches across the top of the pot, and the bottom of the pots measure 2 inches.

When I first bought flower pots for baking, I soaked them for an hour or so in warm water. Then dried them well and coated them with oil liberally and put them into the oven for 30 minutes at 325 degrees. I did this process two or three times before I attempted to bake in them. I have used them for years, and every time I use them I think the bread bakes better. I figure one pot per guest. I use the old-fashioned white bread recipe for the pot bread. I have tried other recipes but this one works best for me. When dinner is ready, I put the pots on the bread and butter plates and pass butter. Sometimes I give them a choice of plain butter, garlic butter or a sweet butter like orange or strawberry.

Old Fashioned Yeast Bread

2 packages dry active yeast
¼ cup warm water
2 cups milk, scalded
6-7 cups flour
½ cup Crisco (room temperature)
½ cup sugar
2 teaspoons salt
¼ teaspoon sugar

In a small cup dissolve the yeast and sugar in the warm water. Put shortening, sugar, and salt in large mixing bowl. Add the yeast mixture and mix well using a wooden spoon. Add flour, 2 cups at a time, and mix well after each addition.

Turn out onto floured board and knead well until smooth and elastic. Turn dough into an oiled bowl and let rise about one hour in warm place until doubled in bulk.

Punch dough down, turn onto board and knead 1 minute and make into 2 loaves. Put into 2 greased 9x5 loaf pans. Brush tops with melted butter or margarine. Cover lightly with waxed paper and let rise in warm place about 45 minutes, or until dough has risen above tops of pans. Bake in preheated 375-degree oven for approximately 40 to 45 minutes. Thump the top of the loaf, and if it sounds hollow it's done. Let set in pans about 5 minutes then turn out on wire rack.

If I'm going to cook the bread in the flower pots, I divide the dough into twelve portions, placing one in each greased flowerpot. Let rise about 30 to 40 minutes until dough reaches above tops of pots. Bake at 375 for about 20 to 25 minutes. Note: The flower pots are hard to handle singly, so I have learned to place them on a large cookie sheet, or better yet the top part of a large broiler pan (with holes in it) the bread cooks better on it.

This is the same recipe that my mother used to make bread by. I started learning to make bread when I was quite young, and I still use this recipe more than any other.

Cynthia's Famous French Bread

1 tablespoon active dry yeast
1 ½ teaspoons sugar
1 ½ cups lukewarm water
3 cups unsifted unbleached flour
1 cup unsifted whole-wheat flour
1 ½ teaspoons salt
Oil
Cornmeal

1. Dissolve yeast and sugar in the lukewarm water.

2. Combine the flours and salt. Add to the yeast mixture, stirring well with wooden spoon.

3. Knead the dough on a lightly floured board until it is no longer sticky. Place the dough in an oiled bowl. Cover and let rise until doubled, about an hour.

4. After dough has doubled in size, punch down and turn it out onto floured board. Divide into two parts. Shape each part into a long narrow loaf.

5. Place the loaves on a greased cookie sheet that has been sprinkled with cornmeal. Cover, let rise about 30 minutes. Using a serrated knife, make shallow slices on the top of each loaf. Bake in pre-heated 400-degree oven for about 25 minutes, until golden brown.

Makes 2 loaves

Cynthia has a tea room in Fredericksburg, Texas and she says they serve this French bread every day at lunch. It is very easy to make and does not take much time or many ingredients. It has a chewy crust and soft inside.

Throwed Rolls

No doubt you have eaten the throwed rolls at Lambert's in Sikeston, Mo. This is their recipe for the rolls.

1 teaspoon sugar
1 package dry active yeast
¼ cup warm water
1 cup warm milk
¼ cup sugar
1 egg, beaten (room temperature)
1 teaspoon salt
4 cups all-purpose flour
¼ cup melted butter

Mix sugar and yeast in ¼ cup warm water, and let stand 5 minutes. In a large bowl, thoroughly mix milk, butter, sugar, egg and salt. Stir in the yeast mixture and 3 ½ cups of the flour, adding a bit more if necessary to make a soft, pliable dough. Turn dough out onto a floured board and let rest while you clean and butter the bowl. Knead dough gently for 4 or 5 minutes, adding flour if necessary, until dough is smooth and silky. Return to buttered bowl, cover with plastic wrap and let rise in warm place until doubled in size. Butter a 12 cup muffin tin. Punch down dough. Preheat oven to 350. Pinch off pieces of dough about 1 ½ inches in diameter (enough to fill a muffin cup) and roll into smooth sphere. Place 2 pieces in each prepared muffin cup (it should be a tight fit). Cover loosely with plastic wrap for 45 minutes, then unwrap and bake 20 to 25 minutes or until light brown. Serve as soon as rolls are cool enough to throw.

Cinnamon Rolls

1 (¼ ounce) package rapid rise yeast
⅓ cup sugar
½ teaspoon salt
3 ½ cups bread flour, divided

¼ cup shortening
¼ cup butter
1 cup boiling water
1 large egg, beaten

Combine yeast, sugar, salt and 2 cups flour in large mixing bowl. Stir together shortening, butter, and 1 cup boiling water until melted. Cool to 120 degrees. Add butter mixture and lightly beaten egg to the flour mixture, and beat for one minute. If you have dough hook attachment for your mixer, attach it now, otherwise continue with regular beaters. Add gradually the rest of the flour, beating well. Cover and let rise in a warm place for 1 hour. Punch down. Divide dough equally. Roll each portion into a 13x9 inch rectangle on a lightly floured surface. Spread with ⅔ cup filling, spread with back of a spoon. Roll up jelly roll fashion. Cut each roll into 16 slices. (An electric knife works well to cut the rolls). Place, cut side up, in buttered 15x10 inch jelly roll pan. Cover and let rise in a warm place for 15 to 20 minutes. Bake at 350 degrees for 20 to 25 minutes. Remove from oven, brush with butter and drizzle with the icing. Continue with the other portion of dough.

Cinnamon Roll Filling

¼ cup butter, softened
½ cup granulated sugar
½ cup firmly packed brown sugar
6 tablespoons all purpose flour
1 ½ tablespoons cinnamon

Combine all ingredients, stirring until well blended.

Note: I sometimes add finely chopped nuts in this filling.

Cinnamon Roll Icing

3 cups powdered sugar, sifted
3 tablespoons milk
½ teaspoon almond flavoring

Stir together until smooth. Spoon icing into a zip-top plastic bag. Snip a corner of bag, and drizzle icing over warm rolls.

Cornmeal Rolls

2 cups milk
¼ cup sugar
¼ cup shortening
¼ cup butter
2 teaspoons salt
1 package dry yeast
¼ cup warm water
2 eggs, beaten
5 to 5 ½ cups all purpose flour, divided
1 ½ cups plain cornmeal
2 tablespoons butter, melted

Combine first five ingredients in a saucepan; heat until shortening and butter melt. Cool to warm (about 110 degrees).

Dissolve yeast in warm water in a large bowl; let stand 5 minutes. Add milk mixture, eggs, and 3 cups flour; beat at medium speed of electric mixer until smooth. Gradually stir in cornmeal and enough remaining flour to make a soft dough. Turn out onto lightly floured board and knead until smooth and elastic. Place in a well-greased bowl, turning to grease top. Cover and let rise in warm place for 1 hour or until doubled. Punch down; shape into 72 small balls. Place 2 balls in each well-greased muffin cup. Cover and let rise in warm place about 1 hour. Bake at 375 degrees for 15 minutes or until golden, brush with melted butter.

Sesame-Wheat Breadsticks

½ cup warm water
1 package dry yeast
2 teaspoons honey
1 tablespoon butter, melted
½ teaspoon salt
¾ cup whole wheat flour
¾ cup all-purpose flour
Vegetable cooking spray
1 large egg, lightly beaten
¼ teaspoon salt
2 tablespoons sesame seeds

Combine first 3 ingredients in a 1 cup measuring cup; let stand 5 minutes. Combine yeast mixture, butter, and salt in a large mixing bowl. Combine flours, and gradually stir 1 ¼ cups flour mixture into yeast mixture. Set remaining ¼ cup flour mixture aside. Place dough in a well-greased bowl, turning to grease top. Cover and let rise in warm place for 1 to 1 ½ hours, until doubled. Turn dough out on floured board. Divide into 15 equal pieces. Roll each piece into a 10-inch stick. Crimp aluminum foil, place on baking sheet, and then lightly coat with cooking spray. Place bread sticks on foil; cover and let rise 1 hour. Combine egg and salt; brush on each breadstick, and sprinkle with sesame seeds. Bake at 400 degrees for 12 minutes. Transfer to wire rack to cool.

Kentucky Ham and Angel Biscuits

1 package dry yeast
½ cup warm water (about 110 degrees)
2 cups buttermilk
4 ½ cups all-purpose flour
1 tablespoon soda
1 teaspoon salt
3 tablespoons sugar
¾ cup shortening
About 3 pounds cooked country ham, thinly sliced

Combine yeast and warm water; let stand 5 minutes. Add buttermilk, and set aside. Combine flour and next 3 ingredients in a large bowl; cut in shortening. Add buttermilk mixture, stirring with a fork until dry ingredients are moistened. Turn biscuit dough onto a lightly floured board, and knead lightly. Roll dough to about ⅓ inch thickness; cut with a 1 ½ inch cutter. Place on a lightly greased baking sheet and bake in preheated 400 degree oven for 10 minutes. Split and fill with ham.

Easy Yeast Rolls

2 packages dry yeast
½ cup warm milk
1 cup milk
½ cup sugar
½ cup shortening, melted
2 large eggs, beaten
1 teaspoon salt
5 ½ cups all-purpose flour
½ cup butter, melted and divided

Dissolve yeast in warm milk, let stand 5 minutes.

Combine yeast mixture, 1 cup milk, sugar, and next 3 ingredients in a large bowl. Gradually add flour, 1 cup at a time, stirring until smooth, continue adding flour to make a soft dough. Place in a well-greased bowl, turning to grease top. Cover with wax paper or a thin towel. Let rise in a warm place about 1 hour until doubled. Turn out on a floured board and knead 5 or 6 times. Divide dough in half. Roll each portion ¼ inch thickness. Cut with a 1 ½ or 2 inch round cutter. Brush rounds with melted butter and fold in half. Place in pan and let rise in warm place for about 1 hour, or until doubled in bulk. Bake at 375 degrees for 15 to 18 minutes. Brush with remaining melted butter.

Corn and Cheese Waffles
with Turkey Hash

1 cup flour
1 cup cornmeal
1 teaspoon baking powder
1 teaspoon salt
¼ teaspoon pepper
¼ teaspoon sugar
1 cup milk
2 eggs
6 tablespoons melted butter
1 ½ cups grated cheddar cheese

Combine, flour, meal, baking powder, salt, sugar and pepper on waxed paper.

In a bowl, beat eggs, milk and butter. Add cheese and stir. Add flour mixture and stir to combine. Pour onto waffle iron (heated) and spread thinly. Makes about six waffles. Serve for brunch or supper with turkey hash.

Turkey Hash

2 tablespoons butter, margarine or chicken fat
2 medium onions, peeled and chopped
2 stalks celery, chopped
¼ pound mushrooms
¼ cup fresh chopped parsley
1 can chicken broth
3 tablespoons flour
4 cups cooked, chopped turkey or chicken

Melt butter in large skillet. Add chopped onions and celery and cook until they begin to brown. Add mushrooms and parsley and stir over high heat about 3 minutes. Combine canned broth with enough water to make 2 cups. Add flour and stir to remove lumps.

Add chicken broth mixture to skillet along with turkey. Bring to a boil and cook until thickened.

Serve over Corn Cheese Waffles. Top with toasted almonds.

Cornmeal Waffles

1 ½ cups self-rising cornmeal
1 ½ cups self-rising flour
¼ cup sugar
3 large eggs, slightly beaten
½ cup milk
1 ½ cup milk
¼ cup butter or margarine, melted

Combine the first three ingredients in a large bowl; make a well in the center of mixture. Combine eggs, milk and butter; add to dry ingredients, stirring just until moistened. Bake in preheated oiled waffle iron. Serve hot with desired toppings.

These waffles make a good supper meal served with Easy Creamed Chicken, and a side dish of Fried Apples.

Plain Waffles

3 eggs, separated
1 ¼ cups milk
1 cup flour
3 teaspoons baking powder
1 teaspoon salt
⅓ cup melted butter

Beat egg whites first and set aside. Mix dry ingredients in bowl. Add egg yolks and milk to melted butter and add to the dry ingredients. Lightly fold in beaten egg whites last.

This is the recipe that my husband, Thomas Tucker, perfected. He liked waffles very much, and he made them most every Sunday morning for our breakfast. He liked lots of melted butter and good sweet syrup.

Moist Pumpkin Bread

⅔ cup shortening
2 ⅔ cups sugar
4 eggs
2 cups cooked, mashed pumpkin
⅔ cup water
3 ½ cups all-purpose flour
½ teaspoon baking powder
2 teaspoons soda
1 ½ teaspoons salt
1 teaspoon cinnamon
1 teaspoon ground cloves
⅔ cup walnuts or pecans, finely chopped
⅔ cup raisins

Cream shortening, gradually add sugar, beating well. Add eggs, mix well. Stir in pumpkin and water. Combine flour, baking powder, soda, salt, cinnamon and cloves; add to creamed mixture, mixing well. Fold in nuts and raisins. Spoon into 2 greased and floured 9x5 loaf pans. Bake at 350 degrees for 1 hour and 10 minutes.

Cheese Muffins

2 tablespoons butter, divided
¼ cup chopped onion
1 ¼ cups biscuit mix
1 cup (4 ounces) shredded sharp American cheese, divided
1 large egg, lightly beaten
½ cup milk
1 tablespoon sesame seeds, toasted

155

Melt 1 tablespoon butter in a skillet on medium heat; add onion and cook, stirring about 3 minutes or until tender. Combine onion, biscuit mix, and ½ cup cheese in a large bowl. Combine egg and milk; add to the onion mixture, stirring just until moistened. Spoon into greased muffin pans, filling half full. Sprinkle with remaining cheese and sesame seeds and dot with remaining butter. Bake at 400 degrees for 12 to 13 minutes or until golden. Serve warm.

Cinnamon Tea Rolls

1 (8 ounce) can refrigerated crescent dinner rolls
2 tablespoons butter, melted
⅓ cup sugar
¼ teaspoon cinnamon
2 tablespoons nuts, very finely ground
Glaze (optional)

Unroll dough onto lightly floured wax paper; press perforation to seal, brush with melted butter. Combine sugar, cinnamon and nuts; sprinkle over dough. Roll up jelly roll fashion, starting at long side; cut into 1-inch slices. Place in lightly greased miniature muffin tins. Bake at 375 degrees for 8 to 10 minutes. Remove from pan and drizzle with glaze. (I personally prefer them without the glaze. Either way they make a nice small sweet.)

Orange Glaze

⅓ cup sifted powdered sugar
1 tablespoon frozen orange juice concentrate, undiluted
1 teaspoon water

Combine all ingredients, stirring until smooth. Drizzle over the rolls.

Poppy Seed Muffins

¾ cup sugar
¼ cup softened butter
½ teaspoon grated orange peel
2 eggs
2 cups all-purpose flour
½ teaspoon salt
¼ teaspoon nutmeg
1 cup milk
½ cup raisins
½ cup chopped pecans
5 tablespoons poppy seeds

Cream butter, sugar and orange peel. Add eggs, one at a time, beating well after each. Combine flour, baking powder, salt and nutmeg. Add to creamed mixture alternately with the milk, beating well after each addition. Fold in raisins, nuts and poppy seeds. Fill muffin tins ¾ full and bake at 400 degrees in a preheated oven for 20 minutes.

Corn Light Bread (quick method)

2 cups cornmeal
½ cup sugar
1 cup flour
1 ½ teaspoons salt
½ teaspoon baking powder
1 teaspoon soda
2 tablespoons shortening, melted
2 cups buttermilk

Mix all dry ingredients together, add buttermilk, a cup at a time. Stir well and add the hot shortening that you melt in the loaf pan that you cook it in. Bake in loaf pan (Pyrex works well) at 350 degrees for 1 hour. Let set in pan 10 minutes before turning out. Serve warm.

I was used to the old-fashioned corn light bread. In fact, my mother and my mother-in-law both made it frequently. This quick recipe is satisfying but not really as tasty as the fermented kind. I settle for it though when I have a meal that it compliments.

Eloise's Angel Cornbread

1 ½ cups cornmeal
1 package dry yeast
1 tablespoon sugar
1 teaspoon salt
1 ½ teaspoons baking powder
1 cup flour
½ teaspoon soda
2 eggs, beaten
2 cups buttermilk
½ cup oil

Combine dry ingredients. Combine eggs, milk and oil. Mix with dry ingredients. Bake in hot greased corn stick irons at 450 degrees for 12-15 minutes. Makes 3 dozen sticks.

This recipe came out of the Bell Notes telephone bill. I think it is a pretty good recipe. Of course the way I like cornbread, it is all good to me!

Hot Water Cornbread
(Corn Dodgers)

2 cups cornmeal
½ teaspoon salt
Boiling water
Oil for skillet plus a bit to put in batter

Put salt in meal; add boiling water and stir. Let it set to swell the meal. Stir in about a tablespoon of the hot oil, and a little milk (this makes it brown better). I shape it with my hands into pones and cook in hot grease in skillet in the oven. This is easier than frying for me. Bake at about 425 degrees, turning once to brown it evenly for about 40 minutes.

Note: I sometimes add an egg. It makes it a bit richer.

Kentucky Spoon Bread

4 cups milk
1 cup white cornmeal
1 ½ teaspoons salt
Pinch sugar
3 tablespoons butter or margarine
4 eggs, beaten

Heat the milk in double boiler over boiling water until tiny bubbles appear around the edges. Gradually add the cornmeal, whisking constantly. Add the salt, sugar and butter. Cook for 10 to 12 minutes or until the butter is melted and the mixture thickens, stirring constantly. Remove from the heat. Add ¼ of the hot mixture gradually to the beaten eggs, add the egg mixture to the remaining hot mixture, stirring constantly. Spoon into a lightly greased 2 quart baking dish or soufflé dish. Bake at 425 degrees for 40 to 45 minutes or until golden brown. Serve with butter.

Chapter Eight - Vegetables

Blessed are those who hunger and thirst for righteousness, for they will be filled. Matthew 5:6

American ways with vegetables have changed in the last couple of centuries. In a 1824 cookbook, the <u>Virginia House Wife</u> by Mary Randolph, it suggests boiling carrots for two hours and steaming broccoli for 30 minutes and roasting potatoes for 2 hours or longer. Now we know that many vitamins are lost when the vegetables are cooked so long. Now most all are suggested to be cooked to the almost tender stage. This chapter shares a variety of vegetable recipes that I hope you and your family can enjoy.

Marinated Asparagus Spears

2 pounds fresh asparagus
½ cup sugar
½ cup cider vinegar
1 teaspoon lemon juice
1 teaspoon salt
¼ teaspoon seasoned pepper

Snap off tough ends of asparagus. Remove scales with a vegetable peeler. Cook asparagus, covered, in boiling water 6 to 8 minutes or until crisp tender; drain, reserving ½ cup liquid. Place asparagus in a large shallow dish or container; set aside.

Combine reserved ½ cup liquid and remaining ingredients in a small saucepan; stir well. Bring to a boil stirring; pour over asparagus. Cover and chill before serving.

Asparagus in Mustard Sauce

1 pound fresh asparagus
½ cup plain yogurt
2 tablespoons Dijon mustard
2 tablespoons mayonnaise
1 tablespoon minced dill weed (fresh)
1 tablespoon minced fresh chives
½ teaspoon fresh ground pepper
½ teaspoon sugar
Lettuce leaves
Cherry tomatoes (optional)

Snap off tough ends of asparagus. Remove scales, if desired. Cook asparagus, covered, in a small amount of boiling water; drain. Place in refrigerator to chill.

Combine yogurt and next 6 ingredients; chill.

Place asparagus on lettuce lined plate, and top with the yogurt sauce. Garnish with cherry tomatoes, if desired.

Sautéed Brussels Sprouts with Almond Butter

2 (10 ounce) cartons brussels sprouts, ends trimmed
3 tablespoons butter
½ cup slivered almonds
3 medium leeks halved lengthwise and sliced crosswise
½ teaspoon salt
½ teaspoon freshly ground pepper

Separate the brussels sprouts into leaves (6 cups approximately) Over high heat, bring a 4 quart pot of salted water to a boil. Add brussels sprouts leaves. When water returns to the boil, boil 2 minutes or until leaves are crisp tender. Drain; reserve leaves in colander.

Meanwhile, in a large skillet, over medium heat, melt 1 tablespoon butter. Add almonds, sauté about 5 minutes or until lightly toasted; drain on paper towel. In same skillet, melt remaining butter. Add the leeks, sauté 6 to 8 minutes or until tender.

To skillet add brussels sprouts leaves, toasted almonds, salt and pepper; cook lifting and tossing mixture with tongs for 2 minutes or until thoroughly heated.

Broccoli

2 packages frozen broccoli
1 cup mayonnaise
1 cup cream, whipped
1 teaspoon sugar
1 teaspoon salt
¼ teaspoon freshly ground pepper
2 eggs, beaten

Cook broccoli in lightly salted water until crisp tender. Drain. Combine remaining ingredients and cover broccoli with sauce in a 9x9 casserole. Bake in preheated 325 degree oven for 25 to 30 minutes.

Broccoli with Horseradish Sauce

1 ½-2 pounds fresh broccoli
¾ cup sour cream
½ teaspoon prepared horseradish
1 ½ teaspoons prepared mustard
Salt and pepper to taste

Wash and trim broccoli. Arrange in steaming rack and steam over boiling water 10-15 minutes. Place on serving dish. Combine remaining ingredients in a small saucepan or microwave dish. Heat thoroughly, stir, spoon over broccoli. Garnish with pieces of pimento.

Sweet and Sour Green Beans

4 cans French style cut green beans
6 slices bacon, fried crisp and crumbled
1 medium onion diced
3 tablespoons pimento
¼ cup vinegar
¼ cup sugar
1 teaspoon salt
¼ cup toasted almonds
Coarse ground pepper

Drain beans; put into a large pan. To the bacon drippings add the vinegar, onion, sugar, pepper and salt. Let come to a boil. Taste for seasonings. Pour over beans and cook about 30 minutes, maybe a little longer. Add pimento, almonds and crumbled bacon just before serving. Serves 12.

Bean Bundles

Cook fresh green beans with carrot and red bell pepper strips in boiling water to cover, until crisp tender. Plunge into cold water to stop the cooking, and drain. Cut yellow squash into ½ inch thick slices and remove the pulp from center of each slice with a round cutter or knife. Secure vegetables in bundles with squash rings, and place in a lightly greased 13x9 inch baking dish. Cover and chill 8 hours, if desired. Drizzle bean bundles with melted butter and bake covered at 350 degrees for 20 to 25 minutes or until thoroughly heated.

Green Bean Roll-Ups

2 cans whole green beans
8 slices bacon
1 clove garlic, pressed
2 teaspoons soft butter
1 teaspoon brown sugar

Drain beans. Put beans in a flat pan. Cook bacon half done; cut each piece into 3 pieces. Mix next three ingredients and drizzle over the 16 to 18 bunches of beans. Roll 1 piece of bacon around each bunch and secure with ½ wooden pick. Arrange the bean bundles in a flat pan or Pyrex and cover with foil and cook in 350 degree oven for 30 minutes. Remove the foil for the last 10 minutes of cooking.

When I serve these on a buffet dinner, I add a small piece of pimento on top of the bacon to add color and decoration.

Southern Creamed Corn in Microwave

 6-8 ears fresh corn
 ¼ cup water
 1-2 teaspoons sugar
 ½ cup butter or margarine, melted
 1 tablespoon cornmeal

Cut corn off the cob and scrape well to remove all of the milk. Place corn in a 1 ½ quart casserole. Add needed amount of water, sugar, butter and cornmeal. Stir well.

Cover with plastic wrap or glass lid. Microwave at high 2 minutes. Stir well and rotate dish. Microwave 3-5 minutes. Stir well. Let stand, covered 2-3 minutes before serving.

Note: The amount of starch in the corn varies, so the amount of water needed may vary (you may need a little more or a little less). I add a little salt after it has cooked.

Celery Casserole

 4 cups celery, sliced
 1 (10 ounce) can cream of chicken soup
 1 can sliced water chestnuts
 ¼ cup pimento
 ¼ cup almonds
 2 tablespoons butter

Cook celery 8 minutes, drain and add the soup, water chestnuts and pimento. Spoon into casserole. Sprinkle crumbs and almonds over top and drizzle with the butter. Bake 35 minutes at 350 degrees.

No Fail Corn Pudding

⅓ cup sugar
3 tablespoons cornstarch
3 tablespoons cornmeal
4 eggs, slightly beaten
2 cans cream style corn
2 cans evaporated milk
4 tablespoons butter
1 teaspoon salt
¼ teaspoon fresh ground pepper
¼ teaspoon nutmeg

Mix sugar, cornstarch and meal. Add eggs and stir; add other ingredients and pour into casserole. Bake at 350 degrees for about 45 minutes.

Hominy and Corn Casserole

3 (15 ½ ounce) cans white hominy, drained
2 (11 ounce) cans white corn, drained
1 (4 ounce) can chopped green chiles, drained
1 tablespoon cornstarch
½ teaspoon ground white pepper
¼ teaspoon salt
1 (8 ounce) container sour cream
1 ½ cups shredded Monterey Jack cheese
1 ½ cups American cheese, shredded
Paprika

Rinse hominy, and drain well. Combine hominy and the next 6 ingredients. Spoon half of hominy mixture into lightly greased 11x7 baking dish. Combine shredded cheeses; sprinkle half of the cheese over casserole. Spoon remaining hominy mixture over cheese.

Baked covered at 350 degrees for 35 minutes or until thoroughly heated. Sprinkle casserole with remaining cheese and paprika and bake uncovered 5 minutes.

Stuffed Mushrooms
(Eddie Sutton's Recipe)

16 large mushrooms, cleaned with stems removed and
    reserved
½ stick butter
3 or 4 finely chopped green onions
1 (16 ounce) can crabmeat (or fresh if available)
Grated Swiss cheese
Grated Parmesan Cheese
Bread crumbs

Sauté crabmeat in butter with green onions using part of mushroom stems. Brush mushroom caps with butter. Fill with mixture of Swiss cheese and crumbs. Stuff and top with parmesan. Bake 350 for 20 to 30 minutes. Serve warm.

Mushroom Pie

Double crust for pie; I don't roll the crust as thin for this pie as I do for a fruit pie.

1 pound mushrooms (canned, sliced and drained)
¼ cup butter
4 tablespoons onion, chopped
¼ cup flour
1 cup beef broth
1 cup whipping cream
Salt and pepper to taste

Sauté first 3 ingredients for 5 minutes. Add flour and cook and stir two minutes. Add the broth and cream; cook on low until thick. Add salt and pepper to taste. Pour into crust and cover with top crust. Bake as 425 degrees for about 45 minutes and brown and bubbly. Let set a few minutes before serving.

NOTE: It is especially good with roast beef

Stuffed Mushrooms

1 ¼ pounds large fresh mushrooms
¼ cup butter or margarine
4 green onions, finely chopped
1/3 cup green pepper, finely chopped
3 tablespoons celery, finely chopped
1 clove garlic, pressed or minced
1 (12 ounce) package frozen spinach soufflé, thawed

Clean mushrooms, remove stems and reserve for other purposes. Melt butter in a skillet. Roll mushroom caps in butter; place in a shallow baking dish, cap side down. Sauté green onion, green pepper, celery and garlic in butter remaining in the skillet; stir in spinach soufflé, and cook until thoroughly heated. Spoon spinach mixture into mushroom caps, cover and bake at 350 degrees for 15 minutes.

Roasted Garlic

Garlic is the IN thing right now. It is good to keep some roasted garlic in the freezer for more instant use.

To roast garlic, cut off the pointed ends of garlic bulbs, and place on a piece of doubled aluminum foil. Drizzle with olive oil and bake at 400 degrees for 1 hour. When it is cooled, the roasted bulbs can be frozen for up to 3 months.

Squeeze the pulp out into butter for a good garlic toast. It is also good to add to vegetables and many meat dishes.

Christmas 2000 – Ethel with buffet including turkey, dressing, ham and Volcano Potatoes

Volcano Potatoes

6 large Idaho potatoes, peeled and quartered
1 (8 ounce) package cream cheese
½ cup sour cream
2 tcaspoons salt
½ teaspoon white pepper
½ cup heavy cream

Cover potatoes with water in a large saucepan. Bring to a boil, cook until tender, about 20 minutes. Drain well. In mixing bowl, mash potatoes. Add cream cheese and beat well; add other ingredients and beat well to the consistency that can be put through a pastry bag with a large tip. Make volcanoes into buttered cookie sheet or shallow pan. Put the caramelized onion slices on top. Heat when ready to serve.

Serves 12

Caramelized Onion Rings:

Slice two large sweet onions ¼ inch thick and spread on a cookie sheet. Sprinkle with a small amount of brown sugar and drizzle melted butter over them. Bake at 325 degrees for about 20 minutes. When they are limp place on top of the mounds (volcanoes) and they will separate into rings. They may be done ahead to this point and when ready to serve drizzle melted butter and place in hot oven to heat and lightly brown.

New Potatoes in Garlic Butter

24 to 30 new potatoes, similar size
1 ½ sticks butter of margarine
4 cloves garlic, pressed

Wash and peel potatoes. Cook in lightly salted water to cover, until barely tender. Drain. Melt butter in a Pyrex dish large enough to have potatoes in a single layer. Sprinkle lightly with salt and turn them over in the garlic butter often as they cook. Bake in 425-degree oven for about 20 to 30 minutes. They should get slightly crusty on outside. Sprinkle with fresh ground pepper and paprika as they cook. Lift carefully with a turner to serving plate and garnish with parsley sprinkled with paprika and garlic powder.

Serves 12

Vegetable Medley

2 celery ribs, chopped
1 medium green pepper, chopped
2 tablespoons onion, chopped
2 tablespoons butter or margarine
3 small zucchini, quartered lengthwise and sliced
1 medium tomato, chopped
1 tablespoon onion soup mix

In a skillet, sauté celery, green pepper and onion in butter for 6 to 8 minutes. Add zucchini, cook and stir over medium heat until tender. Add tomato and soup mix; cook and stir until the tomato is tender

Vegetable Filled Onion Cups

3 medium sweet Spanish onions
3 tablespoons melted butter
1 chicken bouillon cube
½ cup boiling water
1 (10 ounce) package frozen peas
1 (2 ounce) can sliced mushrooms, drained
2 tablespoons chopped pimento
¼ teaspoon marjoram

Peel and halve onions. Place in a large skillet with 1 ½ inches boiling water, salted. Return to boil, then cover and simmer 20 to 25 minutes or until onions are tender. Drain. Remove center sections of onions and chop ¼ cup for filling. Refrigerate or freeze remaining onion from centers to use as needed for soups, stews etc. Brush inside and tops of onions with ½ tablespoon melted butter and keep warm. Meanwhile dissolve chicken bouillon cube in ½ cup boiling water. Add peas and cook 5 minutes. Add mushrooms, pimento, remaining butter, marjoram and reserved chopped onion. Heat well. Spoon vegetables in onion cups and serve.

Vidalia Deep Dish

2 cups water
1 cup uncooked long-grain rice
6 large Vidalia onions
½ cup butter or margarine
2 tablespoons fresh parsley, minced
¼ teaspoon salt

¼ teaspoon white pepper
1 cup shredded Swiss cheese
1 cup whipping cream
Paprika

Bring water to boil in saucepan; add rice. Cover, reduce heat, and simmer 10 minutes. Drain and set aside. Peel and chop onions. Melt butter in Dutch oven over medium heat; add onions and cook 15 minutes stirring often. Remove from heat; stir in rice, parsley, and next 4 ingredients. Spoon mixture into a lightly greased 14x9 casserole. Cover and bake 30 minutes at 350 degrees. Sprinkle lightly with paprika.

Cheesy Mashed Potatoes

6 large potatoes, peeled and quartered
1 (8 ounce) package cream cheese, softened
1 cup shredded cheddar cheese
½ cup sour cream
1 to 2 tablespoons roasted garlic
1 egg
2 teaspoons salt,
¼ teaspoon sugar
½ teaspoon freshly ground pepper

Place potatoes in large saucepan; cover with water. Cover and bring to boil. Cook until very tender or about 25 minutes. Drain well. In mixing bowl, mash potatoes. Add cheese, cream cheese, sour cream, garlic, egg, salt, sugar and pepper; beat until fluffy. Transfer to a greased dish. Cover and bake at 350 degrees for 40 minutes or until heated through. Remove cover last 10 minutes and sprinkle a little more cheese, if desired. Serves 8 to 10

Easy Oven-Baked Potatoes

5 medium potatoes, unpeeled
6 medium onions
½ cup butter or margarine, melted
1 clove garlic, pressed
½ teaspoon salt
¼ teaspoon pepper
¼ teaspoon celery salt
¼ teaspoon paprika

Cut potatoes and onions into ¼ inch slices. Alternate slices, slightly overlapping, in a single layer in a 13x9x2 baking dish. Combine next 5 ingredients; drizzle over potatoes and onion slices. Cover and bake at 400 degrees for 40 minutes.

Sprinkle with paprika and bake, uncovered, for 20 more minutes.

Sliced Baked Potatoes

4 medium baking potatoes
1 teaspoon salt
3 tablespoons melted butter
3 teaspoons mixed herbs
4 tablespoons grated cheddar cheese
1 ½ tablespoons Parmesan cheese

Wash and scrub potatoes. Cut potatoes into thin slices but not all the way through. Put potatoes in baking dish. Fan them slightly. Sprinkle with salt and drizzle with butter and sprinkle herbs. Bake at 425 degrees for about 50 minutes. Remove from oven and sprinkle with cheeses. Bake potatoes for another 10 to 15 minutes until lightly browned and cheeses are melted and potatoes fork tender.

Sweet Potato Pudding

2 cups grated sweet potatoes
1 cup sugar
1 tablespoon flour
2 cups milk
3 eggs, lightly beaten
1 stick butter
1 teaspoon of each cloves, cinnamon and nutmeg
2 tablespoons rum or bourbon
½ cup pecans, chopped

Mix all and put in a casserole and bake 2 hours, stirring every now and then, in 325-degree oven.

This is an old southern recipe from my Aunt Rosa, with whom I stayed in McKenzie, Tennessee when I went to college. She ran the Virginia Hotel, and I worked for her to earn my college expenses and walked the railroad track to the college, along with other local students. Anyway at her hotel, many good foods were served, but the above stands out in my mind as the very best. She served it on Thanksgiving Day and I remember it was so good. I have made it once or twice and it was still good!

Good Sweet Potatoes

5 medium sweet potatoes
¾ cup sugar
1 tablespoon cornstarch
½ teaspoon salt
¼ teaspoon pepper
1 tablespoon orange rind, grated
2 tablespoons butter
1 cup orange juice

Peel and slice sweet potatoes; place in casserole, then place remaining ingredients in a saucepan. Cook over medium heat, stirring until slightly thick. Pour over potatoes and bake covered for 1 hour at 325 degrees.

This one is so simple and so good!

Sweet Potatoes in Orange Shells

6 medium size oranges (thin skin is best)
4 medium sweet potatoes
4 tablespoon orange concentrate, undiluted
3 tablespoons melted butter
½ teaspoon salt
Pinch pepper
1 teaspoon orange flavor (optional)
¼ cup white sugar
¼ cup brown sugar
1 teaspoon cinnamon
3 tablespoons melted butter
3 tablespoon chopped walnuts or pecans

Cut oranges in half, squeeze juice and save for another use. I use a serrated fruit spoon to get the membrane out of the shells. Boil sweet potatoes until tender. Drain. Let cool slightly; peel and mash with the next 6 ingredients. Fill orange shells. Mix next 4 ingredients and put on top of potatoes. Bake at 350 degrees for 15 to 20 minutes. Miniature marshmallows may be added, if desired.

Stuffed Sweet Potatoes

6 medium sweet potatoes
Vegetable oil
1 teaspoon salt
3 tablespoons butter or margarine, softened
1 (6 ounce) can frozen orange juice, thawed and undiluted
1 cup crushed pineapple, drained
½ cup chopped pecans
12 marshmallows

Wash potatoes, and rub with oil. Bake 1 hour at 400 degrees; or until done. Split potatoes lengthwise. Carefully scoop out pulp, leaving shells intact; mash pulp. Add salt, butter, orange concentrate, and pineapple; mix well. Stuff potatoes shells with mixture; sprinkle

175

with pecans. Cut each marshmallow in half; place two halves on each potato. Place potato shells on baking sheet; bake at 400 degrees until slightly brown on top.

Broiled Tomato Halves

1 whole tomato per person, cut in half horizontally
Salt and pepper
½ teaspoon sugar
1 teaspoon dry bread crumbs
Pinch dry basil
1 teaspoon butter

Place the tomato halves cut side up on a lightly greased cookie sheet. Sprinkle with the salt, sugar, pepper and bread crumbs and basil. Dot with butter; place sheet on rack in broiler about four inches from heat. Broil just long enough to melt the butter and slightly brown the crumbs. 1 serving

Oven Fried Green Tomatoes

½ cup cornmeal
½ teaspoon salt
½ teaspoon sugar
¼ teaspoon pepper
1 egg
1 tablespoon water
3 medium size green tomatoes, cut into ¼ inch slices.
Vegetable oil

Combine cornmeal, salt, and pepper, set aside. Combine egg and water; beat well. Dip tomatoes in egg mixture; dredge in cornmeal mixture. Lightly coat a 15x10x1 baking pan with cooking spray. Place tomatoes in a single layer in pan. Bake at 450 degrees for 30 minutes or until golden brown. Sprinkle with the sugar. I use this same method for squash, zucchini and eggplant.

Tomatoes with Okra and Peppers

12 okra pods
1 green pepper, chopped
¼ cup fine bread crumbs
1 tablespoon melted butter or margarine
1 teaspoon minced onion
Salt and pepper
6 medium tomatoes
Buttered breadcrumbs

Wash okra and slice. Parboil 5 minutes. Drain. Mix with green pepper, dry breadcrumbs, butter and onion. Season to taste with salt and pepper.

Core tomatoes, remove tops. Fill with okra mixture. Place in greased baking dish; sprinkle with buttered breadcrumbs, and bake at 375 degrees for 20 minutes. Sprinkle lightly with sugar.

Creamed Turnips

6 to 8 fresh turnips
¼ cup butter
¼ cup sugar
¼ cup heavy cream
½ teaspoon salt
½ teaspoon fresh ground pepper (I use some crushed red
    pepper)

Wash, peel and slice turnips. Boil until tender, and drain well. Add other ingredients, stir well and put into buttered casserole and bake at 375 degrees for 20 to 30 minutes, uncovered. Sprinkle with paprika and a grind of pepper.

Turnips are especially good served with pork chops.

Turnip Greens with Hog Jowl

4 to 5 pounds fresh turnip greens
1 piece hog jowl, about 1 pound

Wash greens well. Put seasoning meat in large kettle with two to three cups of water. Bring to a boil and cook about ten minutes; Lift out of kettle and put the greens into the kettle. Put the meat back on top of greens. Cover and cook on high until they get to boiling, then stir through, reduce heat to simmer and cover.

Let the greens and meat continue to cook for about 45 minutes. Lightly salt and pepper and taste for seasoning. At serving time, lift the greens out of the kettle with a large slotted spoon, onto a platter. I garnish with halved hard boiled eggs and green onions, or sliced sweet onions. Most people like to pour a little vinegar over the greens. People who like them think it is a very fine meal and those who do not like them don't even like to smell them.

Spinach Casserole

1 cup mayonnaise
1 cup heavy cream or evaporated milk
3 eggs lightly beaten
1 tablespoon butter, melted
1 tablespoon flour
½ teaspoon salt
2 cups cooked spinach, chopped

Heat oven to 350 degrees. Combine all ingredients. Pour into buttered casserole. Set in a pan of hot water and bake until firm on top, about 30 to 35 minutes. Serve 6

Plantation Squash

12 medium to small size squash
2 (10 ounce) packages frozen chopped spinach
1 (3 ounce) package cream cheese, softened
3 eggs well beaten
6 tablespoons melted butter
1 ½ tablespoons sugar
½ teaspoon seasoned salt
½ teaspoon onion salt
1 tablespoon coarsely ground pepper
1 cup round buttery cracker crumbs
Paprika
1 pound bacon, cooked crisp and crumbled

Wash squash thoroughly. Drop into hot boiling water; cover and simmer 8 to 10 minutes. Drain and cool slightly; trim off stems. Cut squash in half lengthwise. Scoop out pulp, leaving firm shells; mash pulp.

Cook spinach according to package directions; drain well and add to squash pulp. Add cream cheese, mixing well. Stir in next 6 ingredients; spoon into squash shells. Sprinkle squash with crumbs, paprika and bacon bits. Place on lightly greased baking sheet, cover with foil, and bake at 325 degrees for 30 minutes.

Note: To prepare ahead, spoon filling into squash shells and chill. When ready to bake, sprinkle with crumbs.

Mixed Vegetable Casserole

3 medium to small yellow squash
3 medium to small zucchini squash
1 large sweet onion, cut into 6 to 8 wedges
1-2 tomatoes
2 teaspoons Cavender's spice seasoning
1 teaspoon sugar
2 tablespoons butter

179

Cut squash and zucchini in thick slices or chunks. Cook each until barely tender in a small amount of water in the microwave. Cook the onion wedges the same as squash. Wedge the tomatoes. In a 9x13 baking dish alternate rows of vegetables so there is a yellow, green, white and red. Fill the dish with alternate rows. Melt butter and sugar and drizzle over the vegetables and sprinkle with the Cavender's spice.

Bake at 350 degrees 20 to 30 minutes. Baste two or three times during the cooking with the juices in bottom of casserole. Taste and adjust seasoning if necessary.

This makes a very attractive and tasty vegetable casserole for a buffet dinner or a sit down dinner. It may be prepared early in the day and baked at dinnertime.

Chapter Nine - Desserts

O taste and see that the Lord is good. Psalm 34:8

Pound Cake
From Cissy Greg Files

2 cups butter (no substitute)
3 cups unsifted all-purpose flour
½ teaspoon soda
3 cups sugar
3 tablespoons lemon juice
1 tablespoon vanilla
10 large eggs, separated
¼ teaspoon salt
2 teaspoons cream of tarter

Butter and flour large tube cake pan. Set aside. Sift flour, soda and half the sugar into mixing bowl. Add butter, softened to room temperature, mix until well blended. Add lemon juice, vanilla and egg yolks, one at a time and beat after each. Beat egg whites with salt until soft peaks form. Add remaining sugar gradually and beat well after each addition. Fold cream of tarter in gently. Pour egg whites over the first mixture and fold in well. Pour into pan, and bang on counter top to remove air holes. Put into preheated 325 oven and bake for 1 hour and 15 minutes without opening the door. Then test cake without taking it out of the oven. If done, turn oven off and leave cake in for 15 minutes more or until it shrinks from side of pan. Take cake out of oven and allow to stand in pan for about 10 minutes. Loosen and turn out. The cake keeps well and slices well.

Alabama Lane Cake

7 egg whites
2 cups sugar
⅔ cup butter, softened
1 teaspoon vanilla
3 cups flour (sifted before measuring)
½ cup milk
2 teaspoons baking powder

Sift flour once before measuring, then four more times; add the baking powder the last time; set aside. Cream butter and sugar until light and lemon colored. Add the butter mixture to the flour, alternating with the milk. Add vanilla and fold in the beaten egg whites. Bake in layers at 375 degrees for about 25 minutes. Used greased and floured pans.

Filling for Alabama Lane Cake

7 egg yolks
1 cup sugar
½ cup butter
1 cup seedless raisins, cut fine
1 cup pecans, chopped
1 cup grated coconut
½ cup brandy
½ cup orange juice
½ teaspoon vanilla

Beat egg yolks until light, add sugar gradually and beat until light and lemon colored: add the brandy and orange juice. Meanwhile, melt the butter in top of double boiler, add the egg brandy mixture and stir and stir until it is very thick, about 15 minutes, using a wooden spoon. Remove from heat and add rest of ingredients. Cool and spread between layers of cake. Frost with boiled icing.

Rosalynn Carter's Cake
A Non-Partisan Delight

1 package of white cake mix (dry)
1 (3 ounce) package strawberry gelatin (dry)
¾ cup vegetable oil
4 eggs
2 tablespoons flour
1 cup chopped nuts
1 pint fresh strawberries, sweetened with ½ cup sugar

Mix together the dry cake mix and dry gelatin. Beat well with the oil; add eggs one at a time, beating after each addition and add the nuts that have been mixed with the flour. Add the sweetened strawberries. Mix all well and pour into greased tube pan and bake at 350 degrees for about 50 minutes or when a pick comes out clean. Serve upside down so strawberries will be on top; add whipped cream.

This cake is easy, different and delicious!

Chocolate Italian Cake

5 large eggs, separated
½ cup butter, softened
½ cup shortening
2 cups sugar
2 ¼ cups all-purpose flour
¼ cup cocoa
1 teaspoon baking soda
1 cup buttermilk
1 cup sweetened flaked coconut
⅔ cup finely chopped pecans
2 teaspoons vanilla extract
Chocolate-cream cheese frosting
Garnish: pecan halves or chocolate curls

Beat egg whites at high speed with an electric mixer until stiff peaks form; set aside. Beat butter and shortening until creamy; gradually add sugar, beating well. Add egg yolks, one at a time, beating until blended after each addition. Combine flour, cocoa, and baking soda; add to butter mixture alternately with buttermilk, beginning and ending with flour mixture. Beat at low speed until blended after each addition. Stir in coconut, chopped pecans and vanilla. Fold in egg whites. Pour batter into 3 greased and floured 8 inch round cake pans. Bake at 325 degrees for 25 to 30 minutes or until cake tester comes out clean when inserted in the center. Cool in pans on wire racks for 10 minutes. Remove layers to wire racks, and cool completely. Spread chocolate-cream cheese frosting between layers and on top and sides of cake. Garnish.

Chocolate-Cream Cheese Frosting

1 (8 ounce) package cream cheese, softened
½ cup butter, softened
2 teaspoons vanilla extract
¼ teaspoon cinnamon
1 (16 ounce) package powered sugar
¼ cup unsweetened cocoa
¼ cup buttermilk
⅔ cup finely chopped pecans

Beat first four ingredients at medium speed with and electric mixer until creamy. Combine powered sugar and cocoa; gradually add to butter mixture alternately with buttermilk, beginning and ending with powered sugar mixture. Beat at low speed until blended after each addition. Stir in pecans.

This is a wonderful cake. It is a chocolate version of the well known Italian Cream Cake.

General Robert E. Lee
Orange-Lemon Cake

2 cups sifted cake flour
1 ½ teaspoons baking powder
½ teaspoon cream of tarter
9 eggs, separated
2 cups sugar
½ cup vegetable oil
Grated rind and juice of 1 lemon
Pinch of salt
Orange-Lemon frosting
Garnish: Orange slices and mint leaves

Combine first three ingredients, and sift 6 times; set aside. Combine egg yolks and sugar in a large mixing bowl, beat at high speed until thick and lemon colored. Reduce speed to medium, and gradually add vegetable oil. Add flour mixture; mix until well blended. Stir in lemon rind and juice. Beat egg whites at room temperature and salt until stiff peaks form. Fold whites into batter. Pour batter into 4 wax paper-lined and greased 8 inch round cake pans. Bake at 325 degrees for 20 to 25 minutes or until cake springs back when lightly touched. Cool in pans for 10 minutes. Remove cakes from pans and peel off paper. Cool layer completely on wine racks. Spread orange-lemon frosting between layers and to top and sides of cake. Store in refrigerator. Garnish with orange slices and fresh mint leaves.

Orange-Lemon Frosting

½ cup butter, softened
3 egg yolks
2 (16 ounce) packages powdered sugar, sifted
Grated rind of 4 oranges
Grated rind of 2 lemons
2 tablespoons lemon juice
4 to 5 tablespoon orange juice

Cream butter, add egg yolks and beat well. Add powdered sugar, beating well. Add next 3 ingredients, beating well. Gradually add orange juice.

This Orange-Lemon cake was a favorite of General Robert E. Lee. It has been served at the Beaumont Inn in Harrodsburg, Kentucky for so long that it has become a legendary favorite and it can be ordered from the Inn to be shipped to your chosen destination.

Triple Chocolate Cake

Cocoa
1 (18 ½ ounce) box deep chocolate devils food cake mix
1 (4 ounce) box instant chocolate pudding
¾ cup sour cream
½ cup vegetable oil
½ cup water
½ cup toasted chopped almonds
¼ cup mayonnaise
4 eggs
3 tablespoons almond liqueur
1 teaspoon almond extract
1 cup chocolate chips
Glaze

Preheat oven to 350 degrees. Grease a 10-inch bundt pan and dust with cocoa. Place all ingredients except chocolate chips in large bowl and beat 2 minutes with electric mixer on medium speed. Mix in chocolate chips. Pour into prepared pan. Bake 50 to 55 minutes or until cake tests done. Cool on rack 10 minutes before removing from pan. Place warm cake on serving dish and drizzle with glaze.

Glaze

1 cup powered sugar
3 tablespoons milk
1 teaspoon almond extract

Mix all ingredients thoroughly in small bowl. Let stand at room temperature until ready to glaze cake.

Famous Coconut-Pineapple Cake

1 (15 ¼ ounce) can crushed pineapple in juice, undrained
1 ½ cups butter, softened
3 cups sugar
5 large eggs
½ cup lemon-lime soft drink
3 cups cake flour, sifted
1 teaspoon lemon extract
1 teaspoon vanilla extract
Pineapple filling
Cream cheese frosting
1 (6 ounce) package frozen flaked coconut, thawed

Grease bottom and sides of 3 (9-inch) round cake pans; line bottom with wax paper. Grease and flour the wax paper. Drain pineapple, reserving ¾ cup juice. Remove ¼ cup reserved juice for cream cheese frosting, and reserve crushed pineapple for the pineapple filling. Beat butter at medium speed until creamy; gradually add sugar, beating well. Add eggs, one at a time, beating until blended after each addition. Combine ½ reserved pineapple juice and soft drink. Add flour to butter mixture, beginning and ending with flour. Beat at low speed after each addition. Stir in extracts. Pour into prepared cake pans. Bake at 350 degrees for 25 to 30 minutes or until a tester inserted in center comes out clean. Remove from pans and cool on wire racks. Spread ¾ cup pineapple filling between layers and remaining filling on top of cake. Spread cream cheese frosting on sides of cake; pipe border around top. Sprinkle with coconut.

Pineapple Filling

2 cups sugar
1 cup reserved drained crushed pineapple
¼ cup cornstarch
1 cup water

Stir together sugar and cornstarch in saucepan. Stir in pineapple and water. Cook over low heat, stirring often, for 15 minutes or until thick. Cool.

Cream Cheese Frosting

½ cup butter, softened
¼ cup reserved pineapple juice
1 (3 ounce) package cream cheese, softened
1 teaspoon vanilla extract
1 (16 ounce) package powdered sugar, sifted

Beat butter and cream cheese at medium speed until blended. Gradually add powdered sugar, juice and vanilla, mixing well.

This is one of the cakes that I make for food sales. It usually sells well.

Black Forest Cake

2 cups sifted cake flour
2 cups sugar
¾ cup cocoa
¼ teaspoon baking powder
¾ teaspoon salt
½ cup shortening
½ cup sour cream, divided
½ cup milk
⅓ cup kirsch or other cherry flavor brandy

2 eggs
2 egg yolks
4 cups whipping cream
⅓ cup powdered sugar, sifted
2 tablespoons kirsch
2 (21 ounce) cans cherry pie filling

Combine first 6 ingredients in a large mixing bowl, stir well. Add shortening and ¼ cup of sour cream. Beat at low speed for 30 seconds or until dry ingredients are moistened. Add remaining ¼ cup sour cream, milk, and ⅓ cup kirsch. Beat at medium speed for 1 ½ minutes. Add eggs and egg yolks, one at a time, beating after each addition.

Grease two 9-inch cake pans; line bottoms with wax paper. Grease and flour wax paper and sides of pans. Pour batter into pans. Bake at 350 degrees for 30 to 35 minutes or until wooden pick inserted in center comes out clean. Cool in pans 10 minutes; remove from pans. Peel off wax paper and let cakes cool on racks.

Split cake layers horizontally to make four layers. Break one of the layers into pieces and place in food processor bowl. Top with cover, and pulse a few times until crumbs are made. Set crumbs aside.

Beat whipping cream until foamy; gradually add powdered sugar, beating until soft peaks form. Add 2 tablespoons kirsch, beating until stiff peaks form. Heat the pie filling with 1 tablespoon cornstarch until thick bubbly, stirring while it cooks and thickens. Let cool.

Place 1 cake layer on cake plate; spread with 1 cup whipped cream. Top with 1 cup cherry pie filling, repeat procedure with the third layer. Frost sides and top of cake with whipped cream, reserving 1 ½ cups whipped cream for garnish. Pat cake crumbs generously around sides of frosted cake. Pipe or spoon the remaining whipped cream around top edges of cake; spoon 1 cup pie filling in center. Reserve rest of filling for other uses. Cover and chill cake overnight before serving.

I made this cake recipe one time for the Woman's Club Cake Auction, and it brought $75.

New Basics Coconut Cake

1 cup milk
2 tablespoons unsalted butter
4 eggs
2 cups sugar
2 teaspoons vanilla
2 cups sifted, unbleached all-purpose flour
2 teaspoons baking powder
¼ teaspoon salt

Topping:

6 tablespoons unsalted butter
½ cup plus 2 tablespoons packed brown sugar
4 ounces shredded coconut
1 tablespoon vanilla

Preheat oven to 350 degrees and butter and flour a 13x9 baking pan. In a small saucepan, heat the milk and butter until scalding, but not boiling. Meanwhile, start beating the eggs with the electric mixer. Add the sugar and beat well until thick and foamy. With the beaters on low speed, gradually add the hot milk and vanilla. Sift the flour, baking powder and salt together in a bowl. Beat this into the egg mixture with the mixer on low speed. Pour the batter into prepared pan. Bake for about 30 minutes, or when tester comes out clean. Cool cake slightly in pan. To prepare the topping, melt the butter in saucepan and add brown sugar. Stir in the coconut and vanilla. Spread the coconut mixture over the cake as evenly as possible. Place under the broiler about 6 inches from heat. Broil until topping is bubbling and browned. Watch carefully, it will burn easily.

Angel Food Cake

1 ¼ cups sifted cake flour
½ cup sugar
1 ½ cups egg whites, room temperature (about 12 eggs)
1 ¼ teaspoons cream of tarter
¼ teaspoon salt
1 teaspoon vanilla
¼ teaspoon almond extract
1 ⅓ cups sugar

Measure sifted flour, add ½ cup sugar and sift four times. Combine egg whites, cream of tarter, salt, and flavorings in large bowl. Beat at high speed of electric mixer until soft peaks form. Sprinkle in rest of sugar in 4 additions, beating until blended after each addition. Sift in flour mixture in 4 additions folding in with large spoon, turn bowl often.

Pour into ungreased 10-inch tube pan. Bake at 375 degrees for 35 to 40 minutes. Cool cake upside down in pan on cake rack. Then loosen from sides and remove the cake.

This recipe is by Imogene Stout James. There is more about her and her angel food cakes in the history chapter.

Carrot Cake

2 cups all-purpose flour
1 ½ teaspoon baking soda
1 teaspoon baking powder
¼ teaspoon salt
2 cups sugar
1 ¼ teaspoons ground cinnamon
¾ teaspoon each of ginger and nutmeg
1 ¼ cups vegetable oil
4 eggs, beaten
2 ½ cup shredded carrots
½ cup chopped pecans

1 teaspoon vanilla
Cream cheese frosting
1 (3 ½ ounce) package flaked coconut

Grease and flour three 9-inch round cake pans; line with wax paper and grease it. Combine first 8 ingredients; stir well. Add oil and eggs, beating well at medium speed. Stir in 2 cups shredded carrots, pecans and vanilla. Spoon batter into prepared pans. Bake at 350 degrees for 30-35 minutes. Cool 10 minutes in pans. Remove from pans and peel off wax paper. Let cool completely.

Cream Cheese Frosting

1 (8 ounce) package cream cheese, softened
½ cup butter or margarine, softened
1 (16 ounce) package powdered sugar, sifted
2 teaspoons vanilla
1 to 2 teaspoons milk

Beat cream cheese and butter at medium speed until smooth. Gradually add the powdered sugar until well blended. Stir in vanilla. Add milk as needed for right spreading consistency. Spread frosting between layers and on top and sides of cake. Combine coconut and remaining ½ cup carrots. Toss well. Gently press onto sides and top of cake.

Potluck Pleaser
Lemon Sheet Cake

1 (18 ¼ ounce) package lemon cake mix
4 eggs
1 (15 ¾ ounce) can lemon pie filling
1 (3 ounce) package cream cheese, softened
½ cup butter or margarine, softened
2 cups confectioners sugar
1 ½ teaspoon vanilla

In a large mixing bowl, beat the cake mix and eggs until well blended. Fold pie filling in. Spread into a greased 15x10x1 baking pan. Bake at 350 degrees for 18 to 20 minutes, or until a toothpick inserted in center comes out clean. Cool on wire rack. In a small mixing bowl, beat cream cheese, butter and confectioners sugar until smooth. Stir in vanilla. Spread over cooled cake. Store in refrigerator. Yield 36 squares

The lady who sent it says that the folks love this light but citrus flavor with the pie filling. It's easy to make, and they love the taste.

Apple Cake

2 cups sugar
2 eggs
½ cup water
1 cup corn oil
2 ½ cups peeled and diced apples (about 3 apples)
1 cup nuts, chopped
2 ½ cups flour
2 teaspoons baking powder
1 teaspoon salt
1 teaspoon soda
1 teaspoon cinnamon
2 cups butterscotch chips

Mix sugar, eggs, water and oil in mixer bowl. Sift flour, baking powder, salt, soda and cinnamon. Add dry ingredients and mix on low speed. Stir in apples and nuts. Bake in a 13x9 glass dish, 1 hour at 350 degrees. Sprinkle butterscotch chips when cakes comes out of the oven.

In the fall of 1990, Thomas and I were invited to spend a weekend in the Memphis home of Andre and his wife Patty Roe Saffren. She served this Apple Cake and gave me the recipe. Patty Roe grew up in Marion the daughter of Ladye Roe and Pat Runyan. They now reside in Byhalia, Miss.

White Cake

½ cup Crisco
1 ¾ cups sugar
2 ½ cups cake flour
2 teaspoons baking powder
½ teaspoon soda
½ teaspoon salt
1 ½ cups buttermilk
1 teaspoon vanilla extract
½ teaspoon almond
5 egg whites, beaten stiff

Cream Criso and sugar. Sift flour, baking powder, soda and salt. Add flour mixture alternately with the buttermilk into the Crisco-sugar mixture. Fold egg whites in last. Put into two, nine-inch cake pans lined with greased and floured wax paper. Bake at 350 degrees for 25 minutes.

This cake is good iced with divinity. Seven Minute Frosting, or Sour Cream Frosting with coconut added is also good, as is a chocolate or caramel cream frosting.

Seven-Minute Frosting

2 egg whites
1 ½ cups sugar
¼ teaspoon cream of tarter
1 tablespoon light corn syrup
⅓ cup water

Combine all ingredients in top of double boiler. Place over boiling water and beat with hand mixer until mixture stands in stiff peaks. Scrape bottom and sides of pan occasionally. Add 1 teaspoon of vanilla if desired.

Divinity Icing

2 cups sugar
½ cup water
2 tablespoons white corn syrup
2 egg whites
¼ teaspoon cream of tarter

Put first three ingredients in a saucepan, stir and heat to boiling. Stir and scrape the sugar from sides of pan into the syrup. Boil without stirring until it strings or when the candy thermometer reaches hard boil or 240 degrees. Take off heat. Beat the egg whites and cream of tarter until stiff. Very slowly pour the hot syrup over the egg whites, beating all the while with the electric beater. Continue beating until spreading consistency.

Caramel Frosting

2 cups brown sugar
½ cup cream
1 stick of butter

Let all come to a boil and boil five minutes. Cool and beat until spreading consistency and spread over layers for layer cake or use on a sheet cake also.

White Frosting

3 large egg whites
¼ teaspoon cream of tarter
1 ½ teaspoon vanilla
½ cup cold water
⅛ teaspoon cream of tarter

Put egg whites, vanilla and ¼ teaspoon cream of tarter in mixing bowl. In saucepan, combine water, sugar and ⅛ teaspoon cream of tarter. Simmer, stirring until sugar is dissolved. Boil and brush sides of pan down with cold water. Cook until 230 degrees. Remove from heat. Beat egg whites, ¼ teaspoon cream of tarter and vanilla until soft peeks form. Very slowly pour the syrup into the egg whites, beating all the while. Continue beating about 5 minutes until spreading consistency.

Chocolate Butter Icing

⅓ cup soft butter
3 cups sifted confectioners sugar
3 tablespoons cream
1 ½ teaspoons vanilla
3 (1 ounce) squares unsweetened chocolate, melted

Blend together the soft butter and confectioners sugar; stir in until smooth and the rest of the ingredients. Beat to the spreading consistency.

Prune Cake

3 eggs, beaten
1 cup vegetable oil
1 ½ cups sugar
1 cup buttermilk
½ teaspoon soda
1 teaspoon cinnamon
1 teaspoon nutmeg
1 teaspoon allspice
1 teaspoon vanilla
2 cups flour
1 cup prunes, cooked and cut up
1 cup nuts, chopped

Flour and grease two 9-inch cake pans. Dissolve soda in buttermilk. Mix all the ingredients together and pour into the cake pans. Bake at 300 degrees for 45 minutes. While the cake is baking, make the following sauce.

Sauce:

> 1 cup sugar
> ½ cup buttermilk (dissolve ½ teaspoon soda in it)
> 1 tablespoon white syrup
> ¾ stick butter
> ½ teaspoon vanilla

Boil about 1 minute and pour over the cake while it is warm.

This is a delicious cake!

Key Lime Cheese Cake
with Strawberry Sauce

2 cups graham cracker crumbs
⅓ cup sugar
½ cup butter or margarine, melted
2 (8 ounce) packages cream cheese, softened
1 (8 ounce) Neufchatel cheese, softened
1 ¼ cup sugar
3 large eggs
1 (8 ounce) package sour cream
1 ½ to 2 teaspoons grated lime rind
½ cup lime juice
Garnishes: Whipped cream, strawberry halves

Make crust of first three ingredients. Firmly press on bottom and up sides of a greased 9-inch spring form pan. Bake at 350 degrees for 8 minutes. Beat cheese at medium speed until fluffy; add sugar gradually. Add eggs, one at a time, beating well after each. Stir in sour cream, juice, and rind of lime. Pour batter into crust. Bake at 325 degrees for 1 hour; turn off oven. Partially open door, let stand 15 minutes. Remove from oven and run a knife around edge of pan. Cool completely in pan on wire rack. Cover and chill at least 8 hours. Garnish.

Strawberry Sauce

1 ¼ cup fresh strawberries
¼ cup sugar
1 ½ teaspoons lime rind

Mix together and put on plates at serving time. Decorate cheesecake with strawberry halves and dollop of whipped cream. Put slice on the sauce on the plates.

Almond-Ricotta Cheesecake

2 one-ounce squares semisweet chocolate, chopped and melted
1 cup chocolate wafer cookie crumbs
1 envelope unflavored gelatin
3 tablespoons amaretto liqueur
1 tablespoon cold water
1 cup heavy or whipping cream
¾ cup sugar
2 containers (15 ounces each) ricotta cheese
Garnish: Chocolate curls

Combine melted chocolate and cookie crumbs in bowl. Press in bottom of a 9-inch spring form pan. Freeze until ready to use. Sprinkle gelatin over amaretto and water in 1 cup microwave proof measure; let stand 2 minutes. Microwave on high 40 seconds, stir. Let stand 2 minutes more. In another microwave proof measure, microwave cream on high 45 seconds, until hot. Transfer to blender. With machine on, add gelatin through hole in lid and blend until gelatin is completely dissolved, about 1 minute. Scrap down sides of blender and blend again. Add sugar; blend until dissolved. Add 1 container of ricotta; blend until smooth. Transfer half the mixture to large bowl. Add remaining ricotta cheese to blender and blend until smooth. Stir into bowl. Pour batter into prepared pan. Cover and refrigerate at least 8 hours. To serve, run a small knife around edge of pan. Remove side, garnish with chocolate curls.

German Chocolate Cheesecake

1 cup chocolate wafer crumbs
2 tablespoons sugar
3 tablespoons butter, melted
3 (8 ounce) packages cream cheese, softened
¾ cup sugar
¼ cup cocoa
2 teaspoons vanilla extract
3 large eggs
⅓ cup evaporated milk
⅓ cup sugar
¼ cup butter
Pinch of salt
1 large egg, lightly beaten
½ teaspoon vanilla extract
½ cup chopped pecans
½ cup flaked coconut

Stir together first three ingredients; press into bottom of 9-inch spring form pan. Bake at 325 degrees for 10 minutes. Cool. Beat cream cheese and next three ingredients at medium speed with an electric mixer until blended. Add eggs, one at a time, beating just until blended after each addition. Pour into prepared crust. Bake for 35 minutes. Loosen cake from pan; cool. Chill 8 hours. Stir together evaporated milk and next four ingredients in saucepan. Cook over medium heat, stirring constantly, 7 minutes. Stir in pecans and coconut; spread over cheesecake.

Sweet Potato Cheesecake

1 ¼ cups graham cracker crumbs
¼ cup sugar
¼ cup (½ stick) unsalted butter, melted
2 pounds sweet potatoes
3 (8 ounce) packages cream cheese, softened
¾ cup plus 2 tablespoons sugar

⅓ cup sour cream
¼ cup whipping cream
3 large eggs, room temperature

Topping:

¾ cup firmly packed brown sugar
½ stick unsalted butter
¼ cup whipping cream
1 cup chopped toasted pecans

Mix graham cracker crumbs, 1/4 cup each of sugar and butter together in a small bowl. Press into bottom of a 9-inch spring form pan. Bake 10 minutes. Cool crust completely on wire rack. Bake potatoes 1 hour, cool slightly. Peel. Mash or puree in blender or processor. Transfer 1 ½ cups potatoes to large bowl (reserve any left for another use.)

Add cream cheese, sugar, sour cream and cream and beat until smooth. Add eggs one at a time, blending well after each addition. Pour filling into crust. Bake until tester inserted in center comes out clean, about 1 hour. Turn off oven. Let cake stand one hour with door ajar.

Topping:

Stir sugar and butter in small pan over low heat until sugar dissolves. Increase heat and bring to a boil. Mix in cream, then nuts. Pour hot topping over cheesecake. Refrigerate until cheesecake is well chilled, at least 8 hours. It can be prepared a day ahead.

White Chocolate Cheesecake

¾ cup blanched almonds, ground
¾ cup quick-cooking oats, uncooked
¾ cup graham cracker crumbs
¼ cup sugar
¼ cup plus 2 tablespoons butter, melted

2 (8 ounce) packages cream cheese, softened
1 cup sugar
1 (16 ounce) carton commercial sour cream
1 teaspoon vanilla
8 ounces white chocolate, melted
4 egg whites
⅛ teaspoon cream of tarter
1 tablespoon powdered sugar
Pinch of salt

Combine first five ingredients in a medium bowl; blend well. Press into bottom and 2 inches on sides of a 10-inch spring form pan. Bake at 350 degrees for 5 minutes. Cool on wire rack. Combine cream cheese and 1 cup sugar in a large mixing bowl; beat at medium speed with electric mixer until fluffy. Add sour cream and vanilla; mix well. Stir in white chocolate. Beat egg whites (at room temperature) in a large bowl at high speed with mixer until foamy; add cream of tarter, beating until soft peaks form. Add powdered sugar and continue beating until stiff peaks form. Fold egg whites into cream cheese mixture. Spoon mixture into crumb crust. Bake at 325 degrees for 55 minutes; turn oven off. Leave cheesecake in oven 30 minutes; partially open door of oven, and leave cake in the oven an additional 30 minutes. Cool. Chill 8 hours. Remove from pan. Garnish with dark and light chocolate curls.

White Chocolate Cheesecake

Cheese Cake

2 cups graham cracker crumbs
1 ½ cups sugar
1 stick oleo, melted
1 (8 ounce) package cream cheese
1 package lemon Jell-O
1 tall can Carnation Milk, chilled
1 cup boiling water

Mix graham cracker crumbs and melted oleo and press in a 9x13 pan. (Save ¼ cup of the crumb mixture for the top). Mix Jell-O in boiling water. Let cool. Add sugar to cream cheese and blend well. Pour Jell-O mixture over sugar and cream cheese mixture and blend well. Pour Carnation Milk into a bowl and add 4 teaspoons lemon juice and whip until very stiff. Fold whipped cream into Jell-O cream cheese mixture. Pour into pan on the cracker crust. Top with the remaining crumbs. Chill. Cut into squares.

Fudgy Mint Cheesecake Bars

4 (1 ounce) bars Hershey's unsweetened baking chocolate
10 tablespoons butter or margarine
2 cups sugar
4 eggs
2 teaspoons vanilla
1 cup flour
1 (8 ounce) package cream cheese, softened
1 tablespoon cornstarch
1 (14 ounce) can Eagle Brand Milk
1 teaspoon peppermint flavoring
Green food coloring

Preheat oven to 350 degrees. Melt chocolate with ½ cup butter or margarine. In bowl, combine chocolate mixture with sugar, 3 eggs, vanilla and flour. Spread in greased 9x13 pan. Bake 12 minutes. In mixer bowl, beat cheese, 2 tablespoons butter or margarine and cornstarch until fluffy. Gradually beat sweetened condensed milk then remaining ingredients. Pour over brownie layer. Bake 30 minutes or until set. Top with glaze made as follows: Melt 1 cup (6 ounces) Hershey's semisweet chocolate chips with ½ cup whipping cream, unwhipped. Cook and stir until thickened. Cool, chill and cut into bars.

Fruitcake Cookies

1 cup soft butter
4 cups pecans, chopped
1 ½ cups sugar
1 teaspoon cinnamon
3 eggs, separated
1 teaspoon nutmeg
3 cups flour, divided
½ teaspoon salt
½ pound candied cherries, finely chopped
1 teaspoon vanilla
½ pound candied pineapple, finely chopped
1 teaspoon baking soda, dissolved in a little water
½ pound white raisins

Cream butter; add sugar, then beaten egg yolks. Sprinkle some of the flour over the fruit and pecans. Add spices and salt to remaining flour. Combine butter, fruit and flour mixtures. Add vanilla and soda. Beat egg whites until stiff and fold in. Drop scant teaspoonfuls on greased cookie sheet and bake at 350 degrees for 10-15 minutes. Batter may be prepared several weeks ahead. Freezes well before and after baking. Yield: 125 to 150 cookies.

The above recipe came from Susan Yarbrough several years ago when she was the food editor for The Crittenden Press.

Ultimate Chocolate Brownies

¾ cup Hershey's cocoa
½ teaspoon soda
⅔ cup butter or margarine, melted and divided
½ cup boiling water
2 cups sugar
2 eggs
1 ⅓ cups flour
Pinch salt
1 teaspoon vanilla
1 cup Hershey's semisweet chocolate chips

Heat oven to 350 degrees. Grease 9x13 pan. In medium bowl, combine cocoa and baking soda. Blend ⅓ cup melted butter. Add boiling water; stir until mixture thickens. Stir in sugar, eggs and remaining ⅓ cup melted butter; stir until smooth. Add flour, vanilla and salt; blend completely. Stir in chocolate chips. Pour into prepared pan. Bake 35 to 40 minutes. Cool completely in pan, frost as follows.

One Bowl Butternut Frosting

6 tablespoons butter, softened
½ cup cocoa
2 ⅔ cup confectioners' sugar
⅓ cup milk
1 teaspoon vanilla

In small mixer bowl, cream butter. Add cocoa and confectioners sugar alternately with milk; beat to spreading consistency, blend in vanilla.

Gooey Butter Cookies

½ cup butter
¼ teaspoon vanilla
1 egg
1 (8 ounce) package cream cheese
1 box butter yellow cake mix

Beat butter, vanilla, egg and cream cheese until light and fluffy. Mix in dry cake mix. Preheat oven to 350 degrees. Lightly coat cookie sheet with cooking spray. Drop dough by teaspoonfuls in bowl of powdered sugar, roll into balls. Bake for 12 minutes or until golden.

My young neighbor, Jessie McDowell, gave this recipe to me.

Ladyfingers

Julia Child convinced me a long time ago that I should make Ladyfingers for desserts rather than buy the already baked. They are so easy to make, and as Julia said they are worth the extra time and effort, for they are so much better.

6 eggs, separated
¾ cup sugar
1 cup plus 2 tablespoons flour
½ teaspoon vanilla
Powdered sugar in a sieve or sifter

Butter and flour a baking sheet. Beat egg yolks with ½ cup sugar until stiff. It takes a long time, but it will happen. With clean beaters and bowl, beat egg whites with ¼ cup sugar until stiff peaks form. Set aside. Sift flour into egg yolks and fold quickly to blend. Fold in egg whites. Use a pastry bag to pipe ladyfingers onto cookie sheet. They should be piped about 1 ½ inches wide and four inches long. Sprinkle generously with powdered sugar. Bake at 375 degrees for about 10 minutes. The insides should be dry.

Russian Teacakes

1 cup butter
½ cup sifted powdered sugar
1 teaspoon vanilla
2 ¼ cups flour
¼ teaspoon salt
¾ cup finely chopped nuts

Mix butter, sugar and vanilla thoroughly. Stir in flour and salt. Mix in nuts, chill dough. Heat oven to 400 degrees. Roll dough in 1-inch balls. Place on ungreased baking sheet. Bake 10 to 12 minutes or until set but not brown. While still warm, roll in powdered sugar. Cool. Roll in sugar again.

Italian Almond Kisses

8 ounces almond paste
1 cup sugar
2 egg whites
¼ cup sifted flour
¼ cup confectioners sugar
½ cup finely chopped mixed candied fruit
½ cup slivered almonds
Few grains salt

In medium bowl, use fingers to combine almond paste, sugar and egg whites into a smooth paste. Still kneading, work in flour and confectioners sugar, then the fruit. Drop by teaspoon on lightly greased cookie sheet, two inches apart. Poke a few almonds on top of each cookie. Bake at 300 degrees for 20-25 minutes. Remove cookies immediately and cool on wire rack.

Holiday Hunks

1 cup softened butter
1 ½ cups sugar
3 eggs
1 teaspoon of baking soda dissolved in 2 tablespoons hot
    water
3 cups flour
1 teaspoon cinnamon
1 teaspoon ground cloves
1 pound chopped nuts of choice
1 pound chopped dates
½ cup chopped maraschino cherries
1 pound raisins

Mix sugar and butter until creamy. Add eggs and baking soda and mix. Add flour and spices and mix. Stir in nuts and fruit. Drop by teaspoon onto greased cookie sheet. Bake 350 degrees for about 10 minutes.

This recipe came from "Bell Notes" several years ago. It was reprinted from a cookbook compiled by the Kentucky Chapter of the Telephone Pioneers of America.

Melting Moments

1 cup unsifted flour
½ cup cornstarch
½ cup confectioners sugar
¾ cup corn-oil margarine
1 teaspoon vanilla or almond flavoring

Sift together flour, cornstarch and sugar. In large bowl, beat at medium speed the margarine until smooth. Add flour mixture and flavoring, beat until well blended. Refrigerate 1 hour. Shape into 1-inch balls. Place about 1 ½ inches apart on ungreased cookie sheet; flatten. I use the bottom of a small glass dipped in flour. Bake in 375 degree oven 10-12 minutes. Cool.

This recipe appeared in "Modern Maturity Magazine" in 1985. I have made them ever since.

Chess Tarts

2 cups flour
½ teaspoon salt
½ cup chilled butter, cut into pieces
¼ cup shortening
⅓ cup ice water
2 eggs beaten
1 cup sugar
1 tablespoon cornmeal
2 teaspoons white vinegar
⅓ cup butter or margarine, melted
¼ teaspoon vanilla
Garnish: Fresh berries in season

Combine flour and salt in bowl; cut in ½ cup butter and shortening with pastry blender until mixture resembles course meal. Sprinkle water, one teaspoon at a time over surface; stir with a fork until ingredients are moistened. Shape dough into 36 balls. Place in miniature muffin tins, shaping each ball into a shell. Cover and chill pastry shells 30 minutes. Combine eggs and next five ingredients; stir well. Spoon evenly into pastry shells. Bake at 350 degrees for 20-25 minutes or until golden brown. Remove tarts from pans; let cool on wire racks. Garnish with a berry or mint leaf.

Chocolate Covered Peanut Butter Eggs

2 pounds confectioners sugar
1 medium size jar peanut butter, either smooth or chunky, 18 ounce
16 ounces unsweetened chocolate
½ block paraffin

Mix confectioners sugar and peanut butter in a mixing bowl. I add a small amount of milk. Mold into egg shapes about 1 inch in length, or to desired size. Using a wooden toothpick dip into melted chocolate and paraffin mixture. Let stand until cool on waxed paper. Store in refrigerator.

This recipe was given to me by an acquaintance in Rochester, Minn. She said it was handed down to her from her grandmother who came to this country from Germany.

Pecan Pie Bars

2 cups flour
½ cup sugar
¼ teaspoon salt
¾ cups butter or margarine, cut up
1 cup firmly packed brown sugar
1 cup light corn syrup
½ cup butter or margarine
4 large eggs, lightly beaten
2 ½ cups finely chopped pecans
1 teaspoon vanilla

Combine flour, sugar, and salt in large bowl; cut in ¾ cup butter thoroughly with pastry blender or processor until it resembles crumbs. Press mixture into a greased 9x13 pan. Bake at 350 degrees for 17 to 20 minutes until lightly browned. Combine brown sugar, corn syrup, and ½ cup butter in a saucepan; bring to boil over medium heat, stirring gently. Remove from heat. Stir ¼ of hot mixture into beaten eggs; add the remaining hot mixture. Stir in pecans and vanilla. Pour filling over crust. Bake at 350 degrees for about 30 to 35 minutes or until set. Cool completely in pan on wire rack. Cut into bars.

Old Fashioned Sugar Cookies

1 cup shortening
1 cup sugar
2 eggs
2 tablespoons milk
1 teaspoon vanilla
4 cups sifted flour
2 teaspoons cream of tarter
1 teaspoon soda

Cream shortening and sugar real well. Beat eggs, milk and vanilla; add to sugar mixture. Stir in flour well. Add more if needed. Roll small amount at a time. Roll thin and cut, put on cookie sheet, sprinkle with cinnamon and sugar. Bake at 400 degrees for 8 minutes.

Mrs. Chick gave this recipe to my husband Thomas many years ago. He always thought it was the best sugar cookies he ever tasted, so he made them fairly often, and he would eat far too many while they were still warm.

Peanut Butter Oatmeal Cookies

¾ cup butter flavor Crisco
1 cup peanut butter, chunky
1 ½ cups firmly packed brown sugar
½ cup water
1 egg
1 teaspoon vanilla
3 cups Quaker Oats, either kind
1 ½ cups flour
½ teaspoon baking soda
Granulated sugar

Beat first three ingredients until creamy. Beat in water, egg and vanilla. Add combined dry ingredients; mix well. Cover, chill about two hours. Heat oven to 350 degrees. Shape into small balls. Place on ungreased cookie sheet; flatten with fork dipped in sugar to form crisscross pattern. Bake 9-11 minutes or until edges are golden brown. Cool 1 minute on cookie sheet, remove to wire rack. Cool.

No recipe file would be complete without this old favorite from Quaker Oats.

No-Bake Cookies

2 cups sugar
1 stick of butter
¼ cup cocoa
Pinch of salt
½ cup milk

Cook in heavy saucepan over medium heat. When it starts to boil, cook 3 minutes remove from heat.

Add:

1 teaspoon vanilla
½ cup peanut butter
2 ½ cups quick cook oats

Mix well and drop by spoonful on waxed paper or pour in pan.

Baked Alaska

Baked Alaska

Use a 9-inch round yellow cake for the base. (I usually use a Jiffy cake mix). Put on heat-proof plate or board, and put in freezer. Use rounded bottom mixing bowl that is about 8 inches across the top. Line the bowl with thin plastic wrap, with the edges hanging over the top. Fill the bowl with strawberry ice cream. Place in freezer. A short time before serving make this special meringue. Beat 6 large eggs whites with 1 ½ teaspoons cream of tarter until frothy. Beat in gradually 1 cup sugar. Continue beating until meringue is stiff and glossy. Take the cake and ice cream from freezer; turn the ice cream out onto the cake. Pull off the plastic wrap and quickly spread the meringue onto the ice cream, being sure to seal around the cake. If time permits put back in freezer while you clear the table. Have the oven hot at 500 degrees. Place in oven for about three minutes, until lightly browned. Take to table and serve for a spectacular dessert.

Apricot Almond Soufflé

4 egg whites, room temperature
Pinch of cream of tarter
2 tablespoons almond amaretto
Pinch of salt
2 (4 ¾ ounce) jars strained apricots (baby food)
Whipped cream

Preheat oven to 325 degrees. Butter a 1 quart soufflé dish and sprinkle with sugar. Beat egg whites until foamy. Add cream of tarter and salt; beat until soft peaks form. Gradually add the sugar, beating until stiff. Gently fold in strained apricots and liqueur. Spoon into dish, set in pan of hot water and bake about 40 minutes. Serve warm with whipped cream if desired.

Sweet Potato Cream Brulée

2 medium sweet potatoes, baked, peeled, and mashed
8 large egg yolks
¼ cup brown sugar
1 tablespoon vanilla
1 tablespoon lemon juice
1 quart whipping cream
⅓ cup brown sugar
1 cup sugar
Garnish: chopped toasted pecans

Combine mashed potatoes, ¼ cup brown sugar and lemon juice; spoon mixture into buttered 10 inch deep dish to form a ¼ inch thick layer. Stir together cream, 1 cup sugar, egg yolks and vanilla in medium saucepan. Cook over low heat, stirring constantly, about 5 minutes or until hot. Pour sweet mixture in prepared dish. Place dish in a shallow baking pan. Add hot water to pan to depth of 1 inch. Bake at 325 degrees for 1 hour or until knife inserted in center comes out clean. Remove from water. Cool on wire rack. Cover and refrigerate overnight. Sprinkle with ⅓ cup brown sugar, place custard on jelly roll pan. Broil 5 to 6 inches from heat for about three minutes or until sugar melts. Let harden before serving. Garnish with chopped nuts.

Bread Pudding
from Beaumont Inn
Harrodsburg, Kentucky

1 pound bread, firm French style
3 ¼ cups milk
3 eggs
2 teaspoons vanilla
¾ cup sugar
¼ teaspoon cinnamon
¼ cup pecans
¼ cup raisins

Tear bread into medium pieces. Add sugar and cinnamon. Mix milk, lightly beaten eggs, and vanilla; add to bread mixture. Place ½ in casserole. Layer pecans and raisins. Top with rest of mixture. Bake at 350 degrees for 30 minutes or until lightly brown. Serve warm with sauce (recipe follows).

Bourbon Sauce:

1 cup sugar
6 tablespoons butter, melted
½ cup buttermilk
1 tablespoon bourbon or bourbon flavoring
½ teaspoon soda
1 tablespoon white corn syrup
1 teaspoon vanilla

Mix well; bring to a boil in saucepan and boil for 1 minute. Serve over warm pudding

Microwave Boiled Custard

The Crittenden County Homemakers supplied this recipe several years ago, and I have enjoyed using it so much. I asked their permission to put it in my cookbook, and they granted me the pleasure to share it with you.

2 cups sugar
5 tablespoons cornstarch
½ gallon milk
4 egg yolks
1 teaspoon vanilla

In a 2 ½ quart casserole, mix sugar and cornstarch well. Gradually stir in milk. Microwave on high 15 minutes. Stir well. Microwave on high 8-10 minutes until slightly thickened. Beat egg yolks and gradually stir in some of the cooked mixture. Return egg mixture to casserole, mixing well. Microwave on medium 4 minutes. Stir in vanilla. Cool. I have found that I like to use the hand mixer for the second and third stirrings.

Creamy Rice Pudding

This is the recipe that I used to look forward to eating in the clubhouse dining room at the Kentucky Derby, during the years that I was invited by Thomas' sister and husband, Dorothy and Robert Frazer. It was served very cold, and was so creamy and so good!

2 cups cooked rice
⅓ cup seedless raisins
¼ teaspoon salt
2 ½ cups whole milk, divided
2 tablespoons butter
⅓ cup sugar
2 eggs, beaten
½ teaspoon vanilla

Combine rice, raisins, salt and 2 ¼ cups milk in a saucepan over medium heat 25 to 30 minutes, stirring occasionally. Add butter to hot pudding. Combine sugar, eggs, and remaining ¼ cup milk, add to pudding stirring constantly. Cook 2 to 3 minutes or until mixture thickens, and coats a metal spoon. Remove from heat; add vanilla. Spoon into serving dishes and chill.

Peach Cream Freeze

The cool peach flavor comes from convenient peach pie filling.

1 (22 ounce) can peach pie filling
1 (15 ounce) can sweetened condensed milk
1 (8 ½ ounce) can crushed pineapple, drained
¼ cup lemon juice
¼ teaspoon almond flavoring
Pinch salt
½ cup whipping cream

In a large bowl combine pie filling, sweetened milk, crushed pineapple, lemon juice and almond flavoring. Whip cream; fold into peach mixture. Spoon into a 9x5x4 loaf pan. Freeze. Unmold and slice. Garnish with whipped cream and nuts or cherries. It may be served as individual salads on lettuce leaves. It may also be frozen in individual molds.

Sweet Potato Pie

¼ cup butter or margarine
¼ cup dark corn syrup
¼ cup packed brown sugar
1 tablespoon orange juice
¼ teaspoon salt
½ teaspoon nutmeg
3 eggs, separated
Unbaked 9-inch pie shell
1 ½ cups mashed, cooked or canned sweet potatoes

Cream butter. Blend in sugar and salt and continue to cream until light and fluffy. Blend in egg yolks along with other ingredients, except egg whites. Beat egg whites until stiff but not dry. Fold into sweet potato mixture. Pour into shell and bake in preheated 450-degree oven for 10 minutes. Lower temperature to 350 degrees and bake for 30 minutes longer, or until set. It is best served slightly warm.

Chocolate Meringue Pie

I am listing both my traditional chocolate pie and microwave version as well.

Traditional Chocolate Meringue Pie

1 ¾ cups sugar, divided
2 teaspoons butter, melted and cooled
⅓ cup flour
Pinch of salt
¼ cup cocoa
½ teaspoon cream of tarter
2 cups milk
Baked 9-inch pie shell
4 large eggs, separated

Combine 1 ¼ cups sugar, flour and cocoa in saucepan. Combine milk, egg yolks and melted butter; beat, using wire whisk, until well blended. Gradually add milk mixture to sugar mixture, stirring until smooth. Cook chocolate mixture over medium heat, stirring constantly, until thickened and bubbly (about 10 minutes). Spoon chocolate mixture into pie shell. Set aside. Beat egg whites until foamy; add cream of tarter and beat at high speed, 10 seconds. Continue beating on high adding sugar (remaining ½ cup sugar) very slowly until stiff peaks form and sugar is dissolved. Spread meringue over the filling, being sure to seal well around edge of pastry. Bake at 350 degrees for 10 to 15 minutes until browned lightly.

Microwave Chocolate Meringue Pie
(Same Ingredients)

1 ¾ cups sugar, divided
⅓ cup flour
¼ cup cocoa
2 cups milk
4 large eggs, separated
2 tablespoons butter
½ teaspoon cream of tarter
Pinch of salt
1 baked pastry shell

In a large 8-cup microwave safe cup, mix 1 ¼ cups sugar, flour, cocoa, salt, milk and egg yolks. Beat well with hand mixer. Microwave on high for 3 minutes; stir, microwave five minutes and stir. If it is cooked and thick, remove from microwave; if not, cook a little more. (Microwaves do vary.) Add butter and beat with hand mixer. Pour into baked pastry and set aside. Heat conventional oven to 350 degrees; beat the egg whites with cream of tarter until foamy, gradually add the remaining ½ cup sugar very slowly, beating until stiff peaks form. Spread over the chocolate filling and be sure to seal to edge of pastry. Bake for 10 to 15 minutes, or until lightly browned.

I use the microwave for coconut and lemon pies also.

Lemon Meringue Pie

1 pastry crust, baked
4 large eggs, separated
1 ¼ cups sugar
½ cup fresh lemon juice
½ cup cornstarch
4 tablespoons butter, softened
¼ teaspoon salt
2 teaspoons lemon zest
2 cups water

Meringue:

>4 large egg whites, room temperature
>¼ teaspoon cream of tarter
>⅓ cup sugar

To make the filling: In a medium saucepan, combine sugar, cornstarch and salt, mix well. Gradually stir in the water until mixture is smooth. Heat to boiling over medium heat, stirring constantly, boil 1 minute. Remove from heat. In a small bowl, whisk the egg yolks until blended. Pour in about ½ cup hot cornstarch mixture, stirring until blended. Stir in lemon juice, butter, and lemon zest; mix and pour into cornstarch mixture in pan. Stir to blend. Heat to boiling, stirring constantly. Boil 1 minute, stirring constantly. Pour hot mixture into cooled pastry shell. Preheat oven to 400 degrees. Make meringue: In large bowl of electric mixer, combine the egg whites and cream of tarter and at medium speed, beat until foamy. At high speed, beat in sugar gradually, about two tablespoons at a time. Beat 2 minutes or until stiff peaks form when beaters are raised but meringue is dry and stiff. Spread meringue over hot filling and swirl decoratively. Bake pie 8 to 10 minutes or until top is lightly browned. Cool completely on rack before cutting.

Never Fail Pie Crust

>1 stick oleo
>1 cup flour
>¼ cup ice water

Mix together, chill in a ball wrapped in wax paper. Roll thin and put into pan and fill. If you are baking an empty crust, prick the bottom and sides well with a fork. Bake at 450 degrees about 8-10 minutes.

Geneva Dycus gave me this recipe many years ago, while I was doing some decorating in her home in Dycusburg.

Pie Crust
For Double Crust and Single Crust

1 stick butter (cold) cut into cubes
½ cup Crisco (cold)
½ stick Fleishmans margarine (cold)
3 cups all purpose flour
¼ teaspoon salt
¼ teaspoon sugar
¾ cup ice water

Put first 6 ingredients in food processor or large mixing bowl. Mix until it is like crumbs, then slowly add water and beat just until dough holds together. (It may not take all the water.) Put on lightly floured piece of foil. Press the dough lightly to about a 6-inch circle (it will be thick), and dot with bits of butter or margarine. (I use a total of about 1 tablespoon). Fold dough into a ball, wrap in foil, and refrigerate from an hour to a day. When ready to make pie, divide dough and roll out on lightly floured board till thin. Place in 9- or 10-inch pie plate. Do not stretch dough. Place filling and cover with second crust rolled same as bottom. Place on top and seal the two crusts around edge, brush the bottom edge lightly with water to make the seal. Trim excess and crimp edges. I use the handle of a wooden spoon to make scallop edge. A fork also works well. Then cut some slots in center of top crust for steam to escape. Or top may be cut in strips for lattice.

Apple Pie

Double Crust Pastry
6 tart apples, Wine Sap, Granny Smith, or Red Delicious
½ cup sugar
1 tablespoon flour
¾ teaspoon cinnamon
1 teaspoon lemon juice
Pinch salt
2 tablespoons butter
1 teaspoon vanilla

Peal, core and slice apples. Mix sugar, flour and cinnamon together and lightly mix with apples. Roll crust thin and place in a 9-inch Pyrex dish. Put apples in and dot with butter. Sprinkle the lemon juice and vanilla over top. Cover with a solid top or lattice top. If you use solid top, cut vents in it. Brush top with cream and sprinkle with sugar. Bake at 400 degrees for 1 hour.

Strawberry Rubarb Pie

Double Crust Pastry
1 ½ cups sugar
1 cup strawberries, sliced
⅓ cup flour
2 tablespoons butter
3 cups rhubarb
Pinch salt
Few grains black pepper

Mix sugar, flour and salt; mix lightly through the mixed rhubarb and strawberries. Pour into pastry lined pie dish. Dot with butter. Cover with lattice top crust. Sprinkle with sugar. Bake at 400 degrees for 45-50 minutes.

Nettie York Peach Pie

1 unbaked pie crust
⅓ cup soft butter
6-8 sliced peaches (enough to fill crust)
⅓ cup flour
1 cup sugar
1 egg
1 teaspoon almond flavoring

Fill crust with sliced peaches. Cream the sugar, butter, and flour. Beat in egg and almond. Spread over peaches. Bake 1 hour at 350 degrees.

Nettie York used to cook at the Curve Inn Restaurant many years ago. She served this pie, and I thought it was so delicious and she gave me the recipe.

Bob Andy Pie

1 ½ cups sugar
1 ½ cups milk
¾ cup butter
3 eggs
½ teaspoon cinnamon
2 tablespoons flour
½ teaspoon nutmeg

Mix flour and sugar and cream with butter, add spices, egg yolks and milk. Beat egg whites until stiff and fold into custard. Put into unbaked crust and bake. The egg whites come to the top for a nice topping.

My mother always liked this pie, and she called it an "everyday pie!"

French Silk Pie

3 egg whites, room temperature
1 (4 ounce) package sweet baking chocolate
¼ teaspoon cream of tarter
3 tablespoons water
⅛ teaspoon salt
1 tablespoon brandy
¾ cup sugar
2 cups heavy cream, divided

½ cup chopped pecans or walnuts
Grated sweet chocolate for garnish
½ teaspoon vanilla

Beat egg whites, cream of tarter and salt until foamy. Gradually add sugar, beating until stiff peaks form. Fold in chopped nuts and vanilla. Spoon meringue into well greased 9-inch pie pan. Use a spoon to shape into a pie shell, swirling high around the edge. Bake at 300 degrees for 1 hour. Cool. Combine chocolate and water in a medium saucepan; place over low heat. Cook, stirring often, until chocolate melts. Let cool, stir in brandy. Beat 1 cup whipping cream until stiff peaks form. Fold into chocolate mixture. Pour mixture into meringue shell; chill at lease 4 hours before serving. Beat remaining whipping cream and spread over pie. Garnish with grated chocolate.

This is a bit more time consuming than some pies, but well worth the extra trouble.

Impossible Pie

4 eggs
¼ cup soft butter
2 cups milk
1 teaspoon vanilla
¾ cup sugar
1 cup coconut
½ cup flour

Mix all ingredients in the order given in mixer, on high speed. Pour into greased 10 inch pie pan. Bake at 350 for 35-40 minutes. This pie makes its own crust, filling and topping.

Sweet Potato Cobbler

2 cups raw sweet potatoes, sliced
2 cups water
1 cup sugar
Double crust pie dough
½ teaspoon salt
2 tablespoons butter

Combine potatoes, sugar, salt and water in saucepan. Boil 5 minutes. Cover bottom 9x9 Pyrex baking dish with a thin layer of the dough. Pour potato mixture over pie dough. Cut a few strips of left over dough and drop down into the sweet potato mixture. Dot with the butter. Cover with the other pie crust. Cut vents in crust. Sprinkle top with a little sugar. Bake 375-400 degrees for 25 to 30 minutes.

Peach Cobbler

7 or 8 sliced soft peaches, add water to make a syrup
Few drops lemon juice
1 cup sugar (some peaches sweeter than others)
Pie dough (about 1 ½ single crust recipe)
1 tablespoon corn starch
1-2 tablespoons butter
Pinch of salt
Sprinkle of cinnamon

In medium saucepan mix sugar, cornstarch, salt, lemon, cinnamon and peaches. Bring to a boil and boil for 1 minute. Stir occasionally. Roll dough 1/8 inch thick. Cut a 9x9 square for top. Cut the left over dough in smaller pieces and put in the bottom of a 9x9 Pyrex baking dish. Pour peach mixture into the casserole. Top with the cut up butter. Cover with solid crust or cut the square into strips and make lattice top. If you use the solid top, cut some vents in it. Bake 30 minutes or until top crust is browned at 400 degrees. This cobbler may be made from canned peaches.

Almond Tart

1 stick butter, softened
1 egg
½ cup sugar
1 cup flour
½ teaspoon almond flavoring
⅛ teaspoon salt
1 pkg. instant vanilla pudding

Cream together butter and sugar. Add egg, flour, salt and flavoring. Spread mixture in 9x9 pan. Bake at 350 degrees for 10 to 12 minutes. Cut into squares, but leave in pan to cool. Next step: Prepare one package instant vanilla pudding mix according to package directions. Spread over pastry. Cool. When ready to serve, sprinkle with slivered almonds and crushed strawberries or sliced peaches. Top with whipped cream.

About forty years ago I was privileged to attend the Jurisdictional School of Missions at Lake Junaluska, North Carolina. We stayed at Lambreth Inn and this is one of the dessert recipes that they served. I still serve it. I think it is best with fresh peaches.

Orange Pecan Pie

3 eggs, beaten
½ cup sugar
1 cup dark corn syrup
1 tablespoon grated orange rind
⅓ cup orange juice
1 tablespoon flour
¼ teaspoon salt
1 cup chopped pecans
1 unbaked 9-inch pastry shell
¾ cup pecan halves

Combine first seven ingredients, beat at medium speed of electric mixer until blended. Stir in chopped pecans. Pour into shell. Arrange pecan halves on top. Bake at 350 degrees for 1 hour.

Pumpkin Pie in Pecan Pie Shell
Cissy Gregg 1959

Pecan Pie Crust:

½ cup shortening
1 ¼ cups sifted all purpose flour
1 tablespoon boiling water
½ teaspoon salt
2 tablespoons buttermilk
4 tablespoons chopped pecans

Put shortening in a bowl. Add boiling water and buttermilk and whip with a fork until liquid is absorbed and a thick smooth mixture is formed. Sift flour and salt onto the shortening. Whip and stir into the dough. Work with hands, into a smooth dough. Shape into a flat round. Roll between two squares of waxed paper, into a circle ⅛-inch thick. Peel off top paper, sprinkle 2 tablespoons of pecans. Re-cover with paper and gently roll pecans into dough. Turn pastry over and do the same. Peel off wax paper and place pastry into 9-inch pie pan. Fit pastry into pan, trim ½ inch beyond pan, turn back even with rim. Flute rim. Prick shell with fork. Bake in hot 450 degree oven for 15 to 18 minutes.

Pumpkin Pie

1 ½ cup canned pumpkin
1 teaspoon cinnamon
3 eggs
½ teaspoon ginger
1 cup brown sugar, firmly packed
¼ teaspoon mace
½ teaspoon salt
1 ⅓ cup evaporated milk

Heat pumpkin over low heat, 10 minutes, stirring constantly. Beat eggs slightly in mixing bowl. Stir in brown sugar, salt, spices and pumpkin. Add milk and stir well. Cook as a custard and put into crust. Top with whipped cream or hard sauce at serving time.

Pumpkin Chiffon Pie

1 (10-inch) pie shell, baked
¾ cups milk
2 ¼ cups canned pumpkin
1 ½ cups brown sugar
¼ teaspoon salt
¾ teaspoon ginger
¾ teaspoon cinnamon
½ teaspoon nutmeg
5 eggs, separated
2 envelopes plain gelatin
⅓ cup cold water
1 ½ cup whipping cream, whipped
¾ teaspoon orange rind
⅓ cup sugar

Heat milk and pumpkin in double boiler with brown sugar, salt and spices. Beat egg yokes slightly and add some of hot mixture to the yolks, mixing rapidly. Return to pumpkin mixture and cook until thickened slightly, stirring constantly. Soften gelatin in water, add to custard, stirring until dissolved. Cool until the filling begins to thicken. Beat the egg whites stiff, fold into filling and chill, but don't let it set. Whip cream until stiff with orange rind and sugar. Fold into pumpkin mixture. Chill until quite thick and then put into pie shell. At serving time garnish with sweetened whipped cream.

Chapter Ten - Miscellaneous

*But the fruit of the spirit is love, joy, peace, patience,
kindness, goodness, faithfulness, gentleness
and self-control. Galatians 5:22-23*

Crunch

Brown sesame seed
Rice Crispies Cereal
Pull apart rolls (canned biscuits)
Melted butter

Pull rolls apart, dip in melted butter then in the mixture of Rice Crispies and sesame seeds. Bake at 375 degrees for a few minutes until brown.

Wild Rice Casserole

2 cups uncooked wild rice
½ pound mushrooms
6 slices bacon
½ cup blanched almonds
1 large onion
1 ½ cups consommé
3 stalks celery
½ teaspoon oregano

Soak rice in water overnight. It will swell to about 4 times its original size. Wash well through several waters. Using four cups boiling water for each one of uncooked rice, boil for 5 minutes. Drain and rinse well. Cover with boiling water, add ½ teaspoon salt. Boil 15 minutes using a fork to stir gently as needed. Dice, fry and drain the bacon. Add chopped onion, chopped celery and sliced mushrooms to bacon fat and brown. Place cooked rice in casserole dish. Mix all other ingredients and stir into rice. Salt and pepper to taste. Bake 30 minutes in a 350 degree oven.

Gourmet Wild Rice

⅓ cup currants
2 cups chicken broth
2 tablespoons brandy or sherry
2 tablespoons olive oil
⅔ cup wild rice
⅓ cup pine nuts or pecans or almonds

Combine currants and brandy and set aside. Wash wild rice in three changes of hot water; drain. Combine rice and chicken broth in a medium saucepan; bring to a boil. Cover, reduce heat and simmer 45 minutes or until the rice is tender and the liquid is absorbed. Stir in currant mixture, olive oil, and nuts. Put in casserole and heat in 350 degree oven at serving time.

Scalloped Pineapple

4 cups bread cubes (French, sourdough, or homemade white is best)
1 (20 ounce) can pineapple chunks, drained
3 eggs, beaten
2 cups sugar
1 cup melted butter

Put drained pineapple and bread cubes in baking dish. Mix eggs, sugar and butter together. Pour over pineapple mixture and bake 30 minutes at 350 degrees.

Fried Apples

6 apples
½ stick oleo or butter
½ cup sugar (may need more depending on the apples)
Some red hots, about a dozen to 1 ½ dozen

Wash and peel one strip around center of apples, quarter and core. Cut each quarter into three slices, for average size apples. Put the butter in skillet (I use an electric skillet) heat on medium, put the apples in, pour over the sugar and red hots. Stir through, add a little water and cover. Cook until tender, stirring occasionally. As they become tender, I usually take the lid off to finish the cooking. The red hots help to sweeten and add color to the apples. Different kinds of apples require more sugar and longer time to cook.

Seasoned Crunch Topping

½ cup butter
¼ teaspoon garlic powder
2 cups uncooked quick or old fashioned oats
1 teaspoon oregano
⅓ cup grated Parmesan cheese
½ teaspoon thyme
⅓ cup wheat germ, or chopped nuts
½ teaspoon basil
¼ teaspoon onion salt

Melt butter in a 12x8 microwave proof baking dish on high for 1 minute. Add remaining ingredients; mix well. Microwave on high 8 to 10 minutes or until light brown, stirring every three minutes. Cool. Store in covered container in refrigerator. Makes about 3 ½ cups. Use to top salads instead of croutons. It is also good to top casseroles, vegetables and soups.

Persimmon Pudding

2 cups persimmon pulp
3 eggs
1 ¼ cups sugar
1 to 1 ½ cups all-purpose flour
1 teaspoon baking powder
1 teaspoon soda
½ teaspoon salt
2 teaspoons cinnamon
1 teaspoon ginger
½ teaspoon nutmeg
½ cup butter or margarine, melted
2 ½ cups milk
1 cup raisins, if desired

To prepare persimmon pulp, after washing, pour ½ cup milk over persimmons and let set for 30 minutes. With clean hands, remove seeds from pulp. Beat eggs and sugar into persimmon pulp. Sift dry ingredients together; add alternately with milk to persimmon mixture. Stir in raisins. Bake in a greased, 9x9 inch baking dish in a 325 degree oven for 1 hour or until firm. Top with cream or hard sauce.

This was one of Tom's favorite desserts. He would spot persimmon trees when we were out riding around. The last persimmon pudding I made, Percy Cook got his ladder out and climbed the tree to retrieve persimmons for us. With Tom holding the ladder, Percy shook the tree while I picked up persimmons.

Sauces

Almond Fudge Sauce

3 (3 ounce) squares unsweetened chocolate, chopped finely
½ teaspoon almond extract
1 (14 ounce) can sweetened condensed milk
½ chopped toasted almonds

Heat chocolate and almond extract in heavy saucepan over low heat, stirring often until chocolate is melted and smooth. Pour condensed milk into small bowl. Stir in chocolate mixture. Stir in toasted almonds. Chill. Store in a jar in refrigerator.

Caramel Maple Brickle Sauce

½ cup milk
20 individual caramels
¼ cup maple syrup
½ cup chopped toasted almonds

Combine milk and caramels in pan. Heat over low heat, whisking frequently until caramels are melted and smooth. Stir in maple syrup. Remove from heat and cool. Stir in almonds. Store sauce in refrigerator until ready to use.

Foolproof Hollandaise Sauce

2 egg yolks
1 (3 ounce) cream cheese
2 tablespoons lemon juice
¼ teaspoon salt

Put cream cheese in saucepan, and over medium heat stir in the egg yolks one at a time. Stir in the lemon juice and salt. Cook, stirring until mixture thickens, about four minutes.

Horseradish Apricots

1 can whole apricots, drained
1 (3 ounce) cream cheese, softened
1 teaspoon sugar
1 ½ teaspoons horseradish
Salt and pepper

Remove pits from apricots, drain well. Mix other ingredients and stuff the centers of apricots with mixture. Chill. Serve with ham or turkey.

Garnishes I like

Celery with Red Pepper Ties

Soak celery sticks in butter until limp. Cut red bell pepper in round rings and boil until limp. Tie around the celery sticks. The same can be done with carrot sticks tied with green pepper ties.

Chocolate Garnishes

Chocolate Curls

Try garnishing your cakes with chocolate curls! You will be amazed at how easy they are to make – and how quickly they transform a plain cake into an extra special one!

If you have a solid block of chocolate, just use a vegetable peeler to peel off curls, allowing them to fall gently onto a piece of wax paper or a plate. If you do not have a block of chocolate, then begin by melting chocolate chips or chocolate coating or chocolate bars.

Pour the melted chocolate onto the back of an inverted cookie sheet and spread to a smooth, thin layer. Let cool until firm and pliable but not hard and brittle. Use a cheese slicer, metal spatula or a thin pancake turner to scrape up a thin layer of chocolate using even pressure. The chocolate will curl as you go. The slower you go, the wider the curls will be.

Slide a toothpick through each curl to carefully lift it onto the cake arrangement.

To decorate a casserole, the following are good suggestions:

Cut white bread slices with a three-inch cutter. Brush with a lightly beaten egg, and sprinkle with chopped fresh parsley and diced pimentos. Bake at 350 degrees for 15 minutes or until toasted. Arrange on the top of most any casserole rather than just crumbs.

Another idea: Cut three (two–inch wide) strips of wax paper and even space over casserole. Sprinkle cooked crumbled bacon on four of the uncovered areas. Remove wax paper and sprinkle remaining areas with chopped fresh parsley.

If you are serving a Tex-Mex casserole in a round dish, arrange wax paper strips in spoke fashion over top, spacing evenly. Sprinkle uncovered areas alternately with finely shredded cheese and chopped green onions or chopped fresh cilantro. Remove wax paper and sprinkle remaining areas with ripe olives or diced tomatoes.

I like to keep a simmering pot on a low burner, especially during the holiday season. I use peel from one orange, lime and lemon, two tablespoons whole cloves, two sticks cinnamon broken in two-inch pieces and a bay leaf. Water may be added as it boils down. The decorated pot I use holds about two cups of water. Let it simmer a while and then turn it off. The potpourri scent remains in the house for some time.

Index

About the Author

"From Pilot Knob to Main Street" is not your ordinary cookbook. But then, Ethel Tucker is not your ordinary author. This publication tells a story that has been a lifetime in the making.

The pages herein contain more than blueprints for elegant appetizers, tasty vegetables, dinner parties and unique desserts. What the reader will find is a true taste of Ethel Tucker's penchant for storytelling and preparing fine meals. At age 87, Ethel Tucker has compiled decades worth of recipes and anecdotes that are shared in this cookbook. Years of encouragement from her late husband, Thomas, and friends, eventually prompted her to embark upon this project in 2004.

The author spent nearly all of her life in Crittenden County, Kentucky. This book also recounts Tucker's rearing in the area north of Marion off of Fords Ferry Road known as Pilot Knob, her life as a small-town businesswoman, her long marriage to Thomas Tucker, their entertaining in Crittenden County homes and her involvement in many community and church activities. Indeed, she gives credit for all of her many abilities and blessings to her Lord Jesus Christ.

Ethel Tucker has been described as the "Matriarch of Marion." The accounts, cooking lessons and life's stories contained in this book are testimony to her remarkable character and culinary taste.

Printed in the United States
28720LVS00002B/58-510

9 781420 829594